# THE SCHOMBURG LIBRARY OF
# NINETEENTH-CENTURY BLACK WOMEN WRITERS

*General Editor*, Henry Louis Gates, Jr.

Titles are listed chronologically; collections that include works published over a span of years are listed according to the publication date of their initial work.

Phillis Wheatley, *The Collected Works of Phillis Wheatley*

Six Women's Slave Narratives: M. Prince; Old Elizabeth; M. J. Jackson; L. A. Delaney; K. Drumgoold; A. L. Burton

Spiritual Narratives: M. W. Stewart; J. Lee; J. A. J. Foote; V. W. Broughton

Ann Plato, *Essays*

Collected Black Women's Narratives: N. Prince; L. Picquet; B. Veney; S. K. Taylor

Frances E. W. Harper, *Complete Poems of Frances E. W. Harper*

Charlotte Forten Grimké, *The Journals of Charlotte Forten Grimké*

Mary Seacole, *Wonderful Adventures of Mrs. Seacole in Many Lands*

Harriet Jacobs, *Incidents in the Life of a Slave Girl*

Collected Black Women's Poetry, Volumes 1–4: M. E. Tucker; A. I. Menken; M. W. Fordham; P. J. Thompson; C. A. Thompson; H. C. Ray; L. A. J. Moorer; J. D. Heard; E. Bibb; M. P. Johnson; Mrs. H. Linden

Elizabeth Keckley, *Behind the Scenes. Or, Thirty Years a Slave, and Four Years in the White House*

C. W. Larison, M.D., *Silvia Dubois, A Biografy of the Slav Who Whipt Her Mistres and Gand Her Fredom*

Mrs. A. E. Johnson, *Clarence and Corinne; or, God's Way*

Octavia V. Rogers Albert, *The House of Bondage: or Charlotte Brooks and Other Slaves*

Emma Dunham Kelley, *Megda*

Anna Julia Cooper, *A Voice From the South*

Frances E. W. Harper, *Iola Leroy, or Shadows Uplifted*

Amanda Smith, *An Autobiography: The Story of the Lord's Dealings with Mrs. Amanda Smith the Colored Evangelist*

Mrs. A. E. Johnson, *The Hazeley Family*

Mrs. N. F. Mossell, *The Work of the Afro-American Woman*

Alice Dunbar-Nelson, *The Works of Alice Dunbar-Nelson*, Volumes 1–3

Emma D. Kelley-Hawkins, *Four Girls at Cottage City*

Pauline E. Hopkins, *Contending Forces: A Romance Illustrative of Negro Life North and South*

Pauline Hopkins, *The Magazine Novels of Pauline Hopkins*

Hallie Q. Brown, *Homespun Heroines and Other Women of Distinction*

# Clarence and Corinne;

*or,*
# God's Way

MRS. A. E. JOHNSON

*With an Introduction by*
HORTENSE J. SPILLERS

❧ ❧ ❧

❧ ❧ ❧

*New York    Oxford*
OXFORD UNIVERSITY PRESS
1988

## Oxford University Press

Oxford   New York   Toronto
Delhi   Bombay   Calcutta   Madras   Karachi
Petaling Jaya   Singapore   Hong Kong   Tokyo
Nairobi   Dar es Salaam   Cape Town
Melbourne   Auckland

and associated companies in
Beirut   Berlin   Ibadan   Nicosia

Copyright © 1988 by Oxford University Press, Inc.

Published by Oxford University Press, Inc.,
200 Madison Avenue, New York, New York 10016

Oxford is a registered trademark of Oxford University Press

Library of Congress Cataloging-in-Publication Data

Johnson, A. E., Mrs.
Clarence and Corinne; or, God's way/by Mrs. A.E. Johnson; with
an introduction by Hortense J. Spillers.
p.   cm.—(The Schomburg library of nineteenth-century black
women writers)
Reprint. Originally published: Philadelphia: American Baptist
Publication Society, c. 1890.
I. Title.   II. Title: Clarence and Corinne.   III. Title: God's
way.   IV. Series.
PS2134.J515C5   1988   813'.4—dc19   87-25376
ISBN 0-19-505264-1
ISBN 0-19-505267-6 (set)

The text of *Clarence and Corinne* was reproduced from microfilm
provided courtesy of the Library of Congress.

2 4 6 8 10 9 7 5 3 1

Printed in the United States of America
on acid-free paper

# PUBLISHER'S NOTE

# FOREWORD
## *In Her Own Write*

*Henry Louis Gates, Jr.*

One muffled strain in the Silent South, a jarring chord and a vague and uncomprehended cadenza has been and still is the Negro. And of that muffled chord, the one mute and voiceless note has been the sadly expectant Black Woman, . . . .

The "other side" has not been represented by one who "lives there." And not many can more sensibly realize and more accurately tell the weight and the fret of the "long dull pain" than the open-eyed but hitherto voiceless Black Woman of America.

. . . as our Caucasian barristers are not to blame if they cannot *quite* put themselves in the dark man's place, neither should the dark man be wholly expected fully and adequately to reproduce the exact Voice of the Black Woman.

—ANNA JULIA COOPER, *A Voice From the South* (1892)

The birth of the Afro-American literary tradition occurred in 1773, when Phillis Wheatley published a book of poetry. Despite the fact that her book garnered for her a remarkable amount of attention, Wheatley's journey to the printer had been a most arduous one. Sometime in 1772, a young African girl walked demurely into a room in Boston to undergo an oral examination, the results of which would determine the direction of her life and work. Perhaps she was shocked upon entering the appointed room. For there, perhaps gath-

ered in a semicircle, sat eighteen of Boston's most notable
citizens. Among them were John Erving, a prominent Boston merchant; the Reverend Charles Chauncy, pastor of the
Tenth Congregational Church; and John Hancock, who would
later gain fame for his signature on the Declaration of Independence. At the center of this group was His Excellency,
Thomas Hutchinson, governor of Massachusetts, with An-
drew Oliver, his lieutenant governor, close by his side.

Why had this august group been assembled? Why had it
seen fit to summon this young African girl, scarcely eighteen
years old, before it? This group of "the most respectable
Characters in *Boston*," as it would later define itself, had assembled to question closely the African adolescent on the
slender sheaf of poems that she claimed to have "written by
herself." We can only speculate on the nature of the questions
posed to the fledgling poet. Perhaps they asked her to iden-
tify and explain—for all to hear—exactly who were the Greek
and Latin gods and poets alluded to so frequently in her
work. Perhaps they asked her to conjugate a verb in Latin
or even to translate randomly selected passages from the Latin,
which she and her master, John Wheatley, claimed that she
"had made some Progress in." Or perhaps they asked her to
recite from memory key passages from the texts of John Mil-
ton and Alexander Pope, the two poets by whom the African
claimed to be most directly influenced. We do not know.

We do know, however, that the African poet's responses
were more than sufficient to prompt the eighteen august
gentlemen to compose, sign, and publish a two-paragraph
"Attestation," an open letter "To the Publick" that prefaces
Phillis Wheatley's book and that reads in part:

We whose Names are under-written, do assure the World,
that the Poems specified in the following Page, were (as we

verily believe) written by Phillis, a young Negro Girl, who was but a few Years since, brought an uncultivated Barbarian from *Africa,* and has ever since been, and now is, under the Disadvantage of serving as a Slave in a Family in this Town. She has been examined by some of the best Judges, and is thought qualified to write them.

So important was this document in securing a publisher for Wheatley's poems that it forms the signal element in the prefatory matter preceding her *Poems on Various Subjects, Religious and Moral,* published in London in 1773.

Without the published "Attestation," Wheatley's publisher claimed, few would believe that an African could possibly have written poetry all by herself. As the eighteen put the matter clearly in their letter, "Numbers would be ready to suspect they were not really the Writings of Phillis." Wheatley and her master, John Wheatley, had attempted to publish a similar volume in 1772 in Boston, but Boston publishers had been incredulous. One year later, "Attestation" in hand, Phillis Wheatley and her master's son, Nathaniel Wheatley, sailed for England, where they completed arrangements for the publication of a volume of her poems with the aid of the Countess of Huntington and the Earl of Dartmouth.

This curious anecdote, surely one of the oddest oral examinations on record, is only a tiny part of a larger, and even more curious, episode in the Enlightenment. Since the beginning of the sixteenth century, Europeans had wondered aloud whether or not the African "species of men," as they were most commonly called, *could* ever create formal literature, could ever master "the arts and sciences." If they could, the argument ran, then the African variety of humanity was fundamentally related to the European variety. If not, then it seemed clear that the African was destined by nature to be a slave. This was the burden shouldered by Phillis Wheatley when she successfully defended herself and the authorship of her book against counterclaims and doubts.

Indeed, with her successful defense, Wheatley launched two traditions at once—the black American literary tradition *and* the black woman's literary tradition. If it is extraordinary that not just one but both of these traditions were founded simultaneously by a black woman—certainly an event unique in the history of literature—it is also ironic that this important fact of common, coterminous literary origins seems to have escaped most scholars.

That the progenitor of the black literary tradition was a woman means, in the most strictly literal sense, that all subsequent black writers have evolved in a matrilinear line of descent, and that each, consciously or unconsciously, has extended and revised a canon whose foundation was the poetry of a black woman. Early black writers seem to have been keenly aware of Wheatley's founding role, even if most of her white reviewers were more concerned with the implications of her race than her gender. Jupiter Hammon, for example, whose 1760 broadside "An Evening Thought. Salvation by Christ, With Penitential Cries" was the first individual poem published by a black American, acknowledged Wheatley's influence by selecting her as the subject of his second broadside, "An Address to Miss Phillis Wheatly [*sic*], Ethiopian Poetess, in Boston," which was published at Hartford in 1778. And George Moses Horton, the second Afro-American to publish a book of poetry in English (1829), brought out in 1838 an edition of his *Poems By A Slave* bound together with Wheatley's work. Indeed, for fifty-six years, between 1773 and 1829, when Horton published *The Hope of Liberty*, Wheatley was the *only* black person to have published a book of imaginative literature in English. So central was this black woman's role in the shaping of the Afro-American literary tradition that, as one historian has maintained, the history of the reception of Phillis Wheatley's poetry *is* the history of Afro-American literary criticism. Well into the nineteenth century, Wheatley and the black literary tradition were the same entity.

But Wheatley is not the only black woman writer who stands as a pioneering figure in Afro-American literature. Just as Wheatley gave birth to the genre of black poetry, Ann Plato was the first Afro-American to publish a book of essays (1841) and Harriet E. Wilson was the first black person to publish a novel in the United States (1859).

Despite this pioneering role of black women in the tradition, however, many of their contributions before this century have been all but lost or unrecognized. As Hortense Spillers observed as recently as 1983,

> With the exception of a handful of autobiographical narratives from the nineteenth century, the black woman's realities are virtually suppressed until the period of the Harlem Renaissance and later. Essentially the black woman as artist, as intellectual spokesperson for her own cultural apprenticeship, has not existed before, for anyone. At the source of [their] own symbol-making task, [the community of black women writers] confronts, therefore, a tradition of work that is quite recent, its continuities, broken and sporadic.

Until now, it has been extraordinarily difficult to establish the formal connections between early black women's writing and that of the present, precisely because our knowledge of their work has been broken and sporadic. Phillis Wheatley, for example, while certainly the most reprinted and discussed poet in the tradition, is also one of the least understood. Ann Plato's seminal work, *Essays* (which includes biographies and poems), has not been reprinted since it was published a cen-

tury and a half ago. And Harriet Wilson's *Our Nig,* her
compelling novel of a black woman's expanding consciousness in a racist Northern antebellum environment, never received even *one* review or comment at a time when virtually
*all* works written by black people were heralded by abolition-
ists as salient arguments against the existence of human slav-
ery. Many of the books reprinted in this set experienced a
similar fate, the most dreadful fate for an author: that of
being ignored then relegated to the obscurity of the rare book
section of a university library. We can only wonder how
many other texts in the black woman's tradition have been
lost to this generation of readers or remain unclassified or
uncatalogued and, hence, unread.

This was not always so, however. Black women writers
dominated the final decade of the nineteenth century, perhaps
spurred to publish by an 1886 essay entitled "The Coming
American Novelist," which was published in *Lippincott's
Monthly Magazine* and written by "A Lady From Philadelphia." This pseudonymous essay argued that the "Great
American Novel" would be written by a black person. Her
argument is so curious that it deserves to be repeated:

> When we come to formulate our demands of the Coming
> American Novelist, we will agree that he must be native-
> born. His ancestors may come from where they will, but we
> must give him a birthplace and have the raising of him. Still,
> the longer his family has been here the better he will represent
> us. Suppose he should have no country but ours, no traditions
> but those he has learned here, no longings apart from us, no
> future except in our future—the orphan of the world, he
> finds with us his home. And with all this, suppose he refuses
> to be fused into that grand conglomerate we call the "Amer-
> ican type." With us, he is not of us. He is original, he has
> humor, he is tender, he is passive and fiery, he has been

taught what we call justice, and he has his own opinion about it. He has suffered everything a poet, a dramatist, a novelist need suffer before he comes to have his lips anointed. And with it all he is in one sense a spectator, a little out of the race. How would these conditions go towards forming an original development? In a word, suppose the coming novelist is of African origin? When one comes to consider the subject, there is no improbability in it. One thing is certain,—our great novel will not be written by the typical American.

An atypical American, indeed. Not only would the great American novel be written by an African-American, it would be written by an African-American *woman:*

> Yet farther: I have used the generic masculine pronoun because it is convenient; but Fate keeps revenge in store. It was a woman who, taking the wrongs of the African as her theme, wrote the novel that awakened the world to their reality, and why should not the coming novelist be a woman as well as an African? She—the woman of that race—has some claims on Fate which are not yet paid up.

It is these claims on fate that we seek to pay by publishing The Schomburg Library of Nineteenth-Century Black Women Writers.

This theme would be repeated by several black women authors, most notably by Anna Julia Cooper, a prototypical black feminist whose 1892 *A Voice From the South* can be considered to be one of the original texts of the black feminist movement. It was Cooper who first analyzed the fallacy of referring to "the Black man" when speaking of black people and who argued that just as white men cannot speak through the consciousness of black men, neither can black *men* "fully and adequately . . . reproduce the exact Voice of the Black Woman." Gender and race, she argues, cannot be conflated, except in the instance of a black woman's voice, and it is this voice which must be uttered and to which we must listen. As Cooper puts the matter so compellingly:

> It is not the intelligent woman vs. the ignorant woman; nor the white woman vs. the black, the brown, and the red,—it is not even the cause of woman vs. man. Nay, 'tis woman's strongest vindication for speaking that *the world needs to hear her voice.* It would be subversive of every human interest that the cry of one-half the human family be stifled. Woman in stepping from the pedestal of statue-like inactivity in the domestic shrine, and daring to think and move and speak,— to undertake to help shape, mold, and direct the thought of her age, is merely completing the circle of the world's vision. Hers is every interest that has lacked an interpreter and a defender. Her cause is linked with that of every agony that has been dumb—every wrong that needs a voice.
>
> It is no fault of man's that he has not been able to see truth from her standpoint. It does credit both to his head and heart that no greater mistakes have been committed or even wrongs perpetrated while she sat making tatting and snipping paper flowers. Man's own innate chivalry and the mutual interde-pendence of their interests have insured his treating her cause, in the main at least, as his own. And he is pardonably surprised and even a little chagrined, perhaps, to find his legislation not considered "perfectly lovely" in every respect. But in any case his work is only impoverished by her remaining dumb. The world has had to limp along with the wobbling gait and one-sided hesitancy of a man with one eye. Suddenly the bandage is removed from the other eye and the whole body is filled with light. It sees a circle where before it saw a segment. The darkened eye restored, every member rejoices with it.

The myopic sight of the darkened eye can only be restored when the full range of the black woman's voice, with its own special timbres and shadings, remains mute no longer.

Similarly, Victoria Earle Matthews, an author of short stories and essays, and a cofounder in 1896 of the National Association of Colored Women, wrote in her stunning essay, "The Value of Race Literature" (1895), that "when the literature of our race is developed, it will of necessity be different in all essential points of greatness, true heroism and real Christianity from what we may at the present time, for convenience, call American literature." Matthews argued that this great tradition of Afro-American literature would be the textual outlet "for the unnaturally suppressed inner lives which our people have been compelled to lead." Once these "unnaturally suppressed inner lives" of black people are unveiled, no "grander diffusion of mental light" will shine more brightly, she concludes, than that of the articulate Afro-American woman:

> And now comes the question, What part shall we women play in the Race Literature of the future? . . . within the compass of one small journal ["Woman's Era"] we have struck out a new line of departure—a journal, a record of Race interests gathered from all parts of the United States, carefully selected, moistened, winnowed and garnered by the ablest intellects of educated colored women, shrinking at no lofty theme, shirking no serious duty, aiming at every possible excellence, and determined to do their part in the future uplifting of the race.
>
> If twenty women, by their concentrated efforts in one literary movement, can meet with such success as has engendered, planned out, and so successfully consummated this convention, what much more glorious results, what wider spread success, what grander diffusion of mental light will not come forth at the bidding of the enlarged hosts of women writers, already called into being by the stimulus of your efforts?
>
> And here let me speak one word for my journalistic sisters

who have already entered the broad arena of journalism. Before the "Woman's Era" had come into existence, no one except themselves can appreciate the bitter experience and sore disappointments under which they have at all times been compelled to pursue their chosen vocations.

If their brothers of the press have had their difficulties to contend with, I am here as a sister journalist to state, from the fullness of knowledge, that their task has been an easy one compared with that of the colored woman in journalism.

Woman's part in Race Literature, as in Race building, is the most important part and has been so in all ages. . . . All through the most remote epochs she has done her share in literature. . . .

One of the most important aspects of this set is the republication of the salient texts from 1890 to 1910, which literary historians could well call "The Black Woman's Era." In addition to Mary Helen Washington's definitive edition of Cooper's *A Voice From the South*, we have reprinted two novels by Amelia Johnson, Frances Harper's *Iola Leroy*, two novels by Emma Dunham Kelley, Alice Dunbar-Nelson's two impressive collections of short stories, and Pauline Hopkins's three serialized novels as well as her monumental novel, *Contending Forces*—all published between 1890 and 1910. Indeed, black women published more works of fiction in these two decades than black men had published in the previous half century. Nevertheless, this great achievement has been ignored.

Moreover, the writings of nineteenth-century Afro-American women in general have remained buried in obscurity, accessible only in research libraries or in overpriced and poorly edited reprints. Many of these books have never been reprinted at all; in some instances only one or two copies are extant. In these works of fiction, poetry, autobiography, biography, essays, and journalism resides the mind of the nineteenth-century Afro-American woman. Until these works are made readily available to teachers and their students, a significant segment of the black tradition will remain silent.

Oxford University Press, in collaboration with the Schomburg Center for Research in Black Culture, is publishing thirty volumes of these compelling works, each of which contains an introduction by an expert in the field. The set includes such rare texts as Johnson's *The Hazeley Family* and *Clarence and Corinne*, Plato's *Essays*, the most complete edition of Phillis Wheatley's poems and letters, Emma Dunham Kelley's pioneering novel *Megda*, several previously unpublished stories and a novel by Alice Dunbar-Nelson, and the first collected volumes of Pauline Hopkins's three serialized novels and Frances Harper's poetry. We also present four volumes of poetry by such women as Mary Eliza Tucker Lambert, Adah Menken, Josephine Heard, and Maggie Johnson. Numerous slave and spiritual narratives, a newly discovered novel—*Four Girls at Cottage City*—by Emma Dunham Kelley (-Hawkins), and the first American edition of *Wonderful Adventures of Mrs. Seacole in Many Lands* are also among the texts included.

In addition to resurrecting the works of black women authors, it is our hope that this set will facilitate the resurrection of the Afro-American woman's literary tradition itself by unearthing its nineteenth-century roots. In the works of Nella Larsen and Jessie Fauset, Zora Neale Hurston and Ann Petry, Lorraine Hansberry and Gwendolyn Brooks, Paule Marshall and Toni Cade Bambara, Audre Lorde and Rita Dove, Toni Morrison and Alice Walker, Gloria Naylor and Jamaica Kincaid, these roots have branched luxuriantly. The eighteenth- and nineteenth-century authors whose works are presented in this set founded and nurtured the black women's literary tradition, which must be revived, explicated, analyzed, and debated before we can understand more completely the formal shaping of this tradition within a tradition, a coded literary universe through which, regrettably, we are only just beginning to navigate our way. As Anna Cooper said nearly one hundred years ago, we have been blinded by the loss of sight in one eye and have therefore been unable to detect the full *shape* of the Afro-American literary tradition.

Literary works configure into a tradition not because of some mystical collective unconscious determined by the biology of race or gender, but because writers read other writers and *ground* their representations of experience in models of language provided largely by other writers to whom they feel akin. It is through this mode of literary revision, amply evident in the *texts* themselves—in formal echoes, recast metaphors, even in parody—that a "tradition" emerges and defines itself.

This is formal bonding, and it is only through formal bonding that we can know a literary tradition. The collective publication of these works by black women now, for the first time, makes it possible for scholars and critics, male and female, black and white, to *demonstrate* that black women writers read, and revised, other black women writers. To demonstrate this set of formal literary relations is to demonstrate that sexuality, race, and gender are both the condition and the basis of *tradition*—but tradition as found in discrete acts of language use.

A word is in order about the history of this set. For the past decade, I have taught a course, first at Yale and then at Cornell, entitled "Black Women and Their Fictions," a course that I inherited from Toni Morrison, who developed it in the mid-1970s for Yale's Program in Afro-American Studies. Although the course was inspired by the remarkable accomplishments of black women novelists since 1970, I gradually extended its beginning date to the late nineteenth century, studying Frances Harper's *Iola Leroy* and Anna Julia Cooper's *A Voice From the South*, both published in 1892. With the discovery of Harriet E. Wilson's seminal novel, *Our Nig* (1859), and Jean Yellin's authentication of Harriet Jacobs's brilliant slave narrative, *Incidents in the Life of a Slave Girl* (1861), a survey course spanning over a century and a quarter emerged.

But the discovery of *Our Nig*, as well as the interest in nineteenth-century black women's writing that this discovery generated, convinced me that even the most curious and diligent scholars knew very little of the extensive history of the creative writings of Afro-American women before 1900. Indeed, most scholars of Afro-American literature had never even read most of the books published by black women, simply because these books—of poetry, novels, short stories, essays, and autobiography—were mostly accessible only in rare book sections of university libraries. For reasons unclear to me even today, few of these marvelous renderings of the Afro-American woman's consciousness were reprinted in the late 1960s and early 1970s, when so many other texts of the Afro-American literary tradition were resurrected from the dark and silent graveyard of the out-of-print and were reissued in facsimile editions aimed at the hungry readership for canonical texts in the nascent field of black studies.

So, with the help of several superb research assistants—including David Curtis, Nicola Shilliam, Wendy Jones, Sam Otter, Janadas Devan, Suvir Kaul, Cynthia Bond, Elizabeth Alexander, and Adele Alexander—and with the expert advice of scholars such as William Robinson, William Andrews, Mary Helen Washington, Maryemma Graham, Jean Yellin, Houston A. Baker, Jr., Richard Yarborough, Hazel Carby, Joan R. Sherman, Frances Foster, and William French, dozens of bibliographies were used to compile a list of books written or narrated by black women mostly before 1910. Without the assistance provided through this shared experience of scholarship, the scholar's true legacy, this project could not have been conceived. As the list grew, I was struck by how very many of these titles that I, for example, had never even heard of, let alone read, such as Ann Plato's *Essays*, Louisa Picquet's slave narrative, or Amelia Johnson's two novels, *Clarence and Corinne* and *The Hazeley Family*. Through our research with the Black Periodical Fiction and Poetry Project (funded by NEH and the Ford Foundation), I also realized that several novels by black women, including three works of fiction by Pauline Hopkins, had been serialized in black periodicals, but had never been collected and published as books. Nor had the several books of poetry published by black women, such as the prolific Frances E. W. Harper, been collected and edited. When I discovered still another "lost" novel by an Afro-American woman (*Four Girls at Cottage City*, published in 1898 by Emma Dunham Kelley-Hawkins), I decided to attempt to edit a collection of reprints of these works and to publish them as a "library" of black women's writings, in part so that I could read them myself.

Convincing university and trade publishers to undertake this project proved to be a difficult task. Despite the commercial success of *Our Nig* and of the several reprint series of women's works (such as Virago, the Beacon Black Women Writers Series, and Rutgers' American Women Writers Series), several presses rejected the project as "too large," "too limited," or as "commercially unviable." Only two publishers recognized the viability and the import of the project and, of these, Oxford's commitment to publish the titles simultaneously as a set made the press's offer irresistible.

While attempting to locate original copies of these exceedingly rare books, I discovered that most of the texts were housed at the Schomburg Center for Research in Black Culture, a branch of The New York Public Library, under the direction of Howard Dodson. Dodson's infectious enthusiasm for the project and his generous collaboration, as well as that of his stellar staff (especially Diana Lachatanere, Sharon Howard, Ellis Haizip, Richard Newman, and Betty Gubert), led to a joint publishing initiative that produced this set as part of the Schomburg's major fund-raising campaign. Without Dodson's foresight and generosity of spirit, the set would not have materialized. Without William P. Sisler's masterful editorship at Oxford and his staff's careful attention to detail, the set would have remained just another grand idea that tends to languish in a scholar's file cabinet.

I would also like to thank Dr. Michael Winston and Dr. Thomas C. Battle, Vice-President of Academic Affairs and the Director of the Moorland-Spingarn Research Center (respectively) at Howard University, for their unending encouragement, support, and collaboration in this project, and Esme E. Bhan at Howard for her meticulous research and bibliographical skills. In addition, I would like to acknowledge the aid of the staff at the libraries of Duke University, Cornell University (especially Tom Weissinger and Donald Eddy), the Boston Public Library, the Western Reserve Historical Society, the Library of Congress, and Yale University. Linda Robbins, Marion Osmun, Sarah Flanagan, and Gerard Case, all members of the staff at Oxford, were extraordinarily effective at coordinating, editing, and producing the various segments of each text in the set. Candy Ruck, Nina de Tar, and Phillis Molock expertly typed reams of correspondence and manuscripts connected to the project.

I would also like to express my gratitude to my colleagues who edited and introduced the individual titles in the set. Without their attention to detail, their willingness to meet strict deadlines, and their sheer enthusiasm for this project, the set could not have been published. But finally and ultimately, I would hope that the publication of the set would help to generate even more scholarly interest in the black women authors whose work is presented here. Struggling against the seemingly insurmountable barriers of racism *and* sexism, while often raising families and fulfilling full-time professional obligations, these women managed nevertheless to record their thoughts and feelings and to *testify* to all who dare read them that the will to harness the power of collective endurance and survival is the will to write.

The Schomburg Library of Nineteenth-Century Black Women Writers is dedicated in memory of Pauline Augusta Coleman Gates, who died in the spring of 1987. It was she who inspired in me the love of learning and the love of literature. I have encountered in the books of this set no will more determined, no courage more noble, no mind more sublime, no self more celebratory of the achievements of all Afro-American women, and indeed of life itself, than her own.

# A NOTE FROM
# THE SCHOMBURG CENTER

*Howard Dodson*

The Schomburg Center for Research in Black Culture, The New York Public Library, is pleased to join with Dr. Henry Louis Gates and Oxford University Press in presenting The Schomburg Library of Nineteenth-Century Black Women Writers. This thirty-volume set includes the work of a generation of black women whose writing has only been available previously in rare book collections. The materials reprinted in twenty-four of the thirty volumes are drawn from the unique holdings of the Schomburg Center.

A research unit of The New York Public Library, the Schomburg Center has been in the forefront of those institutions dedicated to collecting, preserving, and providing access to the records of the black past. In the course of its two generations of acquisition and conservation activity, the Center has amassed collections totaling more than 5 million items. They include over 100,000 bound volumes, 85,000 reels and sets of microforms, 300 manuscript collections containing some 3.5 million items, 300,000 photographs and extensive holdings of prints, sound recordings, film and videotape, newspapers, artworks, artifacts, and other book and nonbook materials. Together they vividly document the history and cultural heritages of people of African descent worldwide.

Though established some sixty-two years ago, the Center's book collections date from the sixteenth century. Its oldest item, an Ethiopian Coptic Tunic, dates from the eighth or ninth century. Rare materials, however, are most available for the nineteenth-century African-American experience. It is from these holdings that the majority of the titles selected for inclusion in this set are drawn.

The nineteenth century was a formative period in African-American literary and cultural history. Prior to the Civil War, the majority of black Americans living in the United States were held in bondage. Law and practice forbade teaching them to read or write. Even after the war, many of the impediments to learning and literary productivity remained. Nevertheless, black men and women of the nineteenth century persevered in both areas. Moreover, more African-Americans than we yet realize turned their observations, feelings, social viewpoints, and creative impulses into published works. In time, this nineteenth-century printed record included poetry, short stories, histories, novels, autobiographies, social criticism, and theology, as well as economic and philosophical treatises. Unfortunately, much of this body of literature remained, until very recently, relatively inaccessible to twentieth-century scholars, teachers, creative artists, and others interested in black life. Prior to the late 1960s, most Americans (black as well as white) had never heard of these nineteenth-century authors, much less read their works.

The civil rights and black power movements created unprecedented interest in the thought, behavior, and achievements of black people. Publishers responded by revising traditional texts, introducing the American public to a new generation of African-American writers, publishing a variety of thematic anthologies, and reprinting a plethora of "classic texts" in African-American history, literature, and art. The reprints usually appeared as individual titles or in a series of bound volumes or microform formats.

The Schomburg Center, which has a long history of supporting publishing that deals with the history and culture of Africans in diaspora, became an active participant in many of the reprint revivals of the 1960s. Since hard copies of original printed works are the preferred formats for producing facsimile reproductions, publishers frequently turned to the Schomburg Center for copies of these original titles. In addition to providing such material, Schomburg Center staff members offered advice and consultation, wrote introductions, and occasionally entered into formal copublishing arrangements in some projects.

Most of the nineteenth-century titles reprinted during the 1960s, however, were by and about black men. A few black women were included in the longer series, but works by lesser known black women were generally overlooked. The Schomburg Library of Nineteenth-Century Black Women Writers is both a corrective to these previous omissions and an important contribution to Afro-American literary history in its own right. Through this collection of volumes, the thoughts, perspectives, and creative abilities of nineteenth-century African-American women, as captured in books and pamphlets published in large part before 1910, are again being made available to the general public. The Schomburg Center is pleased to be a part of this historic endeavor.

I would like to thank Professor Gates for initiating this project. Thanks are due both to him and Mr. William P. Sisler of Oxford University Press for giving the Schomburg Center an opportunity to play such a prominent role in the set. Thanks are also due to my colleagues at The New York Public Library and the Schomburg Center, especially Dr. Vartan Gregorian, Richard De Gennaro, Paul Fasana, Betsy

# INTRODUCTION

*Hortense J. Spillers*

All's well that ends well, and *Clarence and Corinne; or, God's Way* by Mrs. A. E. Johnson passionately pursues the formula of happy endings. Incorporated into the revised and corrected social order of the narrative's fictitious town of N————, Clarence and Corinne, the major pair of brothers and sisters in the narrative, are not only financially secure in the end, but also married to another pair of siblings, Bebe and Charley Reade, in a fictional scheme whose outcome the reader successfully anticipates. Running parallel to that tradition of "woman's fiction" described by contemporary feminist inquiry,[1] *Clarence and Corinne* is barely disguised tractarian writing. In other words, the narrative presses its polemical point by way of the story, which provides an occasion for the theme of social uplift.

Nothing, therefore, earmarks this work specifically as one written by a "black woman writer," or an "Afro-American," and except for confirming biographical information on the author, there is little or no evidence in the novel itself to suggest that Amelia E. Johnson wrote according to the putative urgencies of coeval black life in the United States. To that extent, the historic milieu of late nineteenth-century social reform, in which this narrative is situated, overwhelms the problems of race, at least in this particular instance. The reasons, however, why the narrative is packaged in the wrappings of ethnic neutrality and does not address any of the explicit and implied urgencies released by the failures of Reconstruction politics for African-Americans are neither

overly complicated nor far to seek. Amelia Johnson's publishers were clerical "establishment"; in the awful political
climate (for black Americans, at least) of the 1890s,[2] the
power politics of American publishing rested (as they remain)
in the hands of an implacable and dominant majority culture.

   In an important biographical survey exactly contempora-
neous with Amelia Johnson's career, I. Garland Penn observes
that 1889–1890 marked the year for "which [the author]
had been aiming and preparing herself."[3] Mrs. Johnson had
successfully written for publication a manuscript purchased
by the American Baptist Publication Society. According to
the *American Baptist* of Louisville, Kentucky, she became, as
a result, "the first *lady* author whose manuscript had been
accepted by this society" (Penn, p. 424; emphasis mine). We
infer from a notice recorded by Penn from the *Indianapolis
Daily Journal* that Mrs. Johnson's coup qualified her for
redoubled praise, since her contract with the Society also
made her "the first *colored* woman to be thus honored" (Penn,
pp. 424–25; emphasis mine).

   Though Penn provides a careful account of some of the
favorable reviews given to *Clarence and Corinne,* it is only
through the black religious press that we understand more
precisely why the perspective from which this work was
produced appears (to contemporary readers) somewhat odd.
Baltimore's *Baptist Messenger* decided that Johnson's narrative "is one of the silent, yet powerful agents at work to break
down unreasonable prejudice, which is a hindrance to both
races" (Penn, p. 426). From this angle, it is unimportant
exactly *what* and *how* Mrs. Johnson wrote, but altogether
significant *that* she did. Her contemporaries apparently saw
the testimonial, exemplary force of her work as an instance
of sociopolitical weaponry: "The author of 'Clarence and

Corinne' feels confident that there are those among the race who needed only to know that there is a way where there is a will, to follow her example, and *no doubt far surpass this, her first experience in bookmaking;* and she is happy in knowing that come what may, she has helped her people" (Penn, p. 426; emphasis mine).

We cannot tell if the italicized passage from Penn's closing remarks on the subject is ironically truthful or truthfully histrionic, but it is certainly historic: As we look toward the Harlem Renaissance from the vantage of the late nineteenth century, journalism, editing, and "bookmaking" are productively wed, on occasion, in the future of black women's writing in the United States. In the case of Jessie Fauset, Dorothy West,[4] and an Amelia Johnson, for instance, the situation of black women's writing, even the very act of writing itself, is far more important than any particular aesthetic outcome.

Born in 1858 or 1859 (depending on one's sources), Amelia Johnson was educated in Montreal and moved to Baltimore, the native city of her parents, in 1874. Though Monroe Majors,[5] who essentially tracks the same biographical information that Penn offers, locates her birthplace in Baltimore, Penn is less clear on the point, as it seems certain from both biographers that she spent most of her childhood and years of schooling outside the United States. In 1877, she married the Reverend Harvey Johnson, who was the pastor of Baltimore's Union Baptist Church during the closing years of the nineteenth century. Beginning literary work and her marital career at the same time, she first wrote short poems for various black periodicals. Eventually struck by the notion "that there ought to be a journal in which the writers among our people, especially females, could publish stories, poetry, and matter of a purely literary character, for the perusal of young people" (Penn, p. 422), Amelia Johnson initiated *The Joy* in 1887. An eight-page monthly paper, this periodical carried "original stories and poems, and interesting items from a number of exchanges, solicited for the purpose; also, pithy and inspiring paragraphs from the writings of people of our race" (Penn, pp. 423–24).

*The Joy* appears to have been shortlived, since Penn's entry, published a year after *Clarence and Corinne*, already refers to it in the past tense: "and the paper kept up in interest while it lived" (p. 424). Extracts from the *Baltimore Baptist* attested that the contents of *The Joy* were "original, and the general tone very creditable to the editor" (Penn, p. 424). Philadelphia's *National Baptist* customarily reproduced one of her stories, "Nettie Ray's Thanksgiving Day" on its "Family Page" each Thanksgiving for a few years. She launched the "Children's Corner" in Baltimore's *Sower and Reaper,* for which she wrote "The Animal Convention," "The Mignonette's Mission," and "other original contributions" (Penn, p. 424). As the wife of a prominent Baltimore minister, Amelia Johnson must have had ambition to accomplish in writing the sort of Christian witness to which her husband's pulpit gave him immediate access. To that extent, race disappears in *Clarence and Corinne; or, God's Way*, as human community loses specificity, except for its deeply embedded error.

Told in a 187-page manuscript that bears the stamp of the Library of Congress, *Clarence and Corinne* was copyrighted April 21, 1890. A didactic narrative of the family, the story asserts its historical specificity in unmistakable ways. The reform programs of the late century's women's movement in the United States are everywhere evident in the narrative's systematic injunction against "demon" alcohol and its destructive effects on the nuclear family. The dangers that alcoholism poses to women as wives and mothers, and to their children in particular, constitute the major premise of this fiction. If *Clarence and Corinne* lends itself at all to a simplified descriptive apparatus, we can say without doubt that the work is vividly syllogistic. A male-headed household not only centers on the father as the linchpin of economic well-being, but also as the primary source of familial law and order. An irresponsible head-of-house inevitably invites doom on the entire family unit: Other family personalities are exposed to a series of interconnected disasters, including the effects of an enervated mother figure and the interruption for children of the normal order of human and social development.

Isolated from their peers, Clarence and Corinne are early school dropouts because they do not have sufficiently attractive clothes to ward off the taunts of other youths. Once exposed to the wolves of hunger and deprivation brought on by the father's failures, the family goes into decline as the children are uprooted and turned out into the world. Clarence and Corinne are orphaned before our very eyes, subjected to the sufferance of others and shuttled from one pair of hands to another.

The children of "heartless Jim" Burton and his wife, whom the narrative identifies only as "Mrs. Burton," Clarence and Corinne are in the prime of childhood and essentially remain there, in a timeless zone of innocence, until suddenly, in the penultimate chapter of the work, they come of age and independence. The narrative opens with a description of their poverty, also evinced in the condition of the cottage in which they live. Mrs. Burton, who never leaves the chair in which she is passively poised in the opening scene, has lost all interest in herself, her children, and her household because the available resources are wasted in support of the father's drinking habit. For no ostensible reason beyond what is already spelled out, Mrs. Burton dies early one morning, sitting in the customary chair, and is first discovered by Corinne, as the drunken father/husband sleeps fitfully, thrown across the bed in full dress. We later learn that Mrs. Burton succumbs to a "heart condition," but we are also asked to infer that the probable causes of a "bad" heart are malnutrition, disappointment, and the violence of spiritual, physical, and psychic abuse. Burton leaves the scene abruptly; the municipality will bury Mrs. Burton, and the children are parceled out to various guardians.

In response to his sister's lachrymose outburst—"why did mother die?"—Clarence both answers the question and provides the argumentative engine that drives the text:

> How could she live, battered and beaten, and starved as she was, and by our father too; the one who could have made us all comfortable and happy. But instead of that he's made us miserable—no, it wasn't him, either; it was that dreadful, dreadful stuff, whisky. Yes, drink ruined our father, and now it's killed our mother; and nobody cares for us because we're the children of a drunkard. (p. 19)

Not only could *Clarence and Corinne* have been written, theoretically, under the auspices of the Women's Christian Temperance Union, but it might have served quite well—as it did, in fact—the aims of most Protestant organizations, including the national Sunday school movement. It is altogether appropriate, then, that the work was published by the American Baptist Publication Society.

According to the *Missionary Visitor* of Toulon, Illinois, the narrative was the "first Sunday-school library book written by a colored author" (Penn, p. 425). "Well-adapted to the intermediate classes of Sunday-school readers," Johnson's work was said to be "healthy in tone" (Penn, p. 425). The *Baptist Teacher* echoes the religious journal of Toulon in noting that, "as the first Sunday-school book published from the pen of a colored writer," the narrative acquires "special interest" (Penn, p. 425). Penn, observing that these sympathetic reviews come from "members of the white race," goes on to say that "the book was written from affection for the [black] race, and loyalty to it, the author desiring to help demonstrate the fact that the colored people have thoughts of their own, and only need suitable opportunities to give them utterance . . ." (pp. 425–26). As Mrs. Johnson's readers—black and white—smuggle in race, the narrative's subtitle insinuates its own supplementary meanings. *God's Way* renders the *other* theme of the work, and even though introduced secondarily, it provides the complementary moral of this heuristic and exemplary demonstration.

Although there is little need to recapitulate more of the story's plot, we might briefly observe certain narrative "symptoms" that generate it. Once dispatched to their respective guardians, Clarence and Corinne fall into good and bad hands, respectively. Clarence becomes Dr. Barrett's "boy," or young factotum, who begins his career holding the good doctor's horse. Wishing to reestablish his now-blighted household and provide a home for his sister, Clarence soon leaves the beneficent employ of Barrett, seeking his fortunes in the city of L————. Corinne, on the other hand, fares poorly in this schematic narrative economy, falling into the hands of Rachel Penrose, who is stingy, unfair, and so abusive in overworking the child that she induces the conditions of ill health leading to Corinne's extended sickness. But as the narrative pits the endurance of its young protagonists against a world of motherless and unnurtured adults, it also projects a cast of "helpers," who, scattered along the children's trajectory of fall into misadventure and renewal, offer them such momentary sustenance as to move them along to the next point.

Corinne's protracted illness and Clarence's separation from his sister and departure from N——— only seem unfortunate when, in reality, both moves are necessary for the literal and figurative salvation of the characters. Clarence succeeds in the new town until snared in false accusation by a jealous and resentful coworker. Corinne cannot remain with Helen and Mary Gray, the sisters who rescued her from the meanness and hypocrisy of Rachel Penrose. Eventually going to live with Uncle Nathan and Aunt Anna Stone (the half-sister of the Grays' deceased father) at Brierton's Sweetbrier Farm, Corinne does not know that forlorn Clarence is only miles away from the city. But in time Clarence is brought to the home of Sweetbrier's Rev. Reade, his children Charley and Bebe, and his widowed sister Patty. There, not only is Clarence reunited with Corinne, but in that reunion a four-way match occurs: The Reade children and the young Burtons will become close friends and companions, as the girls go off to boarding school together and the boys do likewise. Clarence is so successful that he finally studies medicine and becomes *Dr.* Burton, who reclaims the property on which the cottage of his early years once stood, providing, in the fulfillment of his old wish, a new home for his beloved sister.

Because these child protagonists each discovers *"God's* way" through their adversity, the future unfolds providentially

before them, and its crucial signs are marriage and reconcil-
iation. Perfectly paired with the persons who are, in effect,
their gender doubles, Clarence and Corinne have their cake
and eat it too. They find in Charley and Bebe Reade the
brother and sister they never had, as well as the divinely
appointed bride and groom. By a well-planned detour, the
Burtons as family are regenerated as husband/wife, who also
function *like* brother/sister.

The story takes place in a twice-fictitious spatial order. On
the one hand, N——— and L——— sustain no geo-
graphical identity that we can posit, even in imaginative
terms. On the other hand, these unlocatable places are anywhere and everywhere, throwing an allegorical coloring over
the whole. Time in this narrative is similarly undifferentiated,
for the Clarence and Corinne of the inaugural pages are the
Clarence and Corinne of the closing, minus the "Conclusion."
Time, therefore, is not elaborated here in a chronological or
temporal order that is marked by interior rhythms of character, but is tracked unprogressively, as "one damn thing
after another." Clarence and Corinne discover not only "God's
way," but also His time, which apparently operates according
to some arbitrary and hidden logic. The story ends when
adversity runs out, an ending that apparently comes about
because God has ordained it, having answered at last the
sincere prayers of the good Gray women. Time is fulfilled,
as in the "fulness of time." It does not fructify, or "grow,"
and reveal; we experience character only as the manipulated
weights and valences of an already prescribed outcome.

For every misdeed, there is a narrative action that corrects
it in exact ratio and proportion. For Sam Baker, the "bad
guy" who frames Clarence, and for Mr. Emory, their employer, who believes that Clarence has stolen money from

him, there is Mother Carter, who opens her home to the hurt and embittered boy. For the *wrong* "Mrs. Stone," there is the comical Jack and the gruff Jonathan Banks, who deliver Corinne to the *right* "Mrs. Stone" and the correct Stone house of Brierton. Even though letters misfire and messages go awry, we never worry for long that there is not an opposite corrective order running alongside the current of adversity. The work hardly qualifies as tragic and cannot be called a comic tale in any precise way, but it is designed to turn out well for some and *correctly* for everyone. James Burton is killed by a runaway horse and wagon; his children read about his death and public expiation in the local newspapers. Mr. Emory learns the truth about the lie told on Clarence because bad Sam confesses. Rachel Penrose dies as she has lived— alone and stinting, even though Corinne shows her care and attention in the end. Fragile Mary Gray succumbs to illness and dies, while her tenacious sister Helen, her strong arm and support, lands a husband. In this strict narrative economy of reward and punishment, people take their place according to the motives that are assigned them, their justice meted out "poetically."

Even though *Clarence and Corinne* does not answer any of the expectations of a post-modernist reading protocol, it is a type of story that we must learn to read again for precisely that reason. Neither ambiguity nor the trap of the subtext seems at all relevant to this tale whose moral is outright. In fact, a critic or reviewer is anxious to get the *right* pitch here, because literary analysis appears to be too much effort or not enough. In trying to adjust my own reading of this text, I now understand more fully why its illustrations and the story it tells bring on a vague sense of *déjà vu*. Having spent my childhood, in part, "practicing" language and reading in the Baptist Sunday school system of Memphis, I recognize the ways and means of this tale at a level of readerly response that precedes the critical. In a very real sense, Johnson's story is touched by the anonymous, its authorship somewhat beside the point, for we could easily encounter it and stories like it in the preacher's exemplum, the reformer's plea, and the journalist's zeal to situate a new, urbanized American in the quickened sociologies of the wayward city. This narrative offers an extended exhortation to a new social order, now urged to bind up the wounds of its battered women, its broken children. In that way—astonishingly—the United States of a full century ago appears less foreign than we are disposed to imagine.

# NOTES

1. Among other works on communities of women writers, two are especially relevant to literary production by women in the nineteenth century: Nina Baym, *Woman's Fiction: A Guide to Novels by and about Women in America, 1820–1870* (Ithaca: Cornell University Press, 1978); and Jane Tompkins, *Sensational Designs: The Cultural Work of American Fiction, 1790–1860* (New York: Oxford University Press, 1985).

2. Paula Giddings' important research sketches the political background of national events that affected the lives of African-Americans, and the particular role of black women's reform efforts in the emerging drama: *When and Where I Enter: The Impact of Black Women on Race and Sex in America* (New York: William Morrow, 1984).

3. *The Afro-American Press and Its Editors*. Rpt. The American Negro: His History and Literature, William Loren Katz, gen. ed.

(New York: Arno Press and the New York Times, 1969), p. 424. (All further references to this source will be included in the text.)

4. Though it is generally known that Jessie Fauset served as an editor at *Crisis* magazine, house organ of the NAACP, during W. E. B. Du Bois' tenure there, the reader should see sources on the Harlem Renaissance period for systematic information: David Levering Lewis, *When Harlem Was In Vogue* (New York: Vintage Books, 1982); and Jervis Anderson, *This Was Harlem 1900–1950* (New York: Farrar Straus Giroux, 1982).

See also Dorothy West, *The Living is Easy* (reprint ed., with an afterward by Adelaide M. Cromwell; Old Westbury: The Feminist Press, 1982). West's brief adventure with her own journal, *Challenge*, which went through only five issues, is told here (pp. 350–63).

5. Dr. Monroe A. Majors, *Noted Negro Women: Their Triumphs and Activities* (Chicago: Donohue and Henneberry, 1893). Rpt. The Black Heritage Library Collection from the Fisk University Library Negro Collection, 1971 (p. 210).

# Clarence and
# Corinne

Clarence and Corinne.

Page 7.

# CLARENCE AND CORINNE;

BY

Mrs. A. E. JOHNSON.

PHILADELPHIA:

1420 CHESTNUT STREET.

# CLARENCE AND CORINNE;

OR,

# GOD'S WAY.

BY

Mrs. A. E. JOHNSON.

PHILADELPHIA :
AMERICAN BAPTIST PUBLICATION SOCIETY,
1420 Chestnut Street.

# CONTENTS.

---

# CLARENCE AND CORINNE.

---

## CHAPTER I.

### DISCOURAGED.

ON the outskirts of the pretty town of N——, among neat vine-covered homes, like a blot upon a beautiful picture, there stood a weather-beaten, tumble-down cottage.

Its windows possessed but few unbroken panes, and rags took the place of glass. The rough door hung on a single hinge, which was so rusty as almost to refuse to perform its duty for the paintless boards that hung upon it for support. There was a little garden plot in front, separated from the street by broken palings, and a gate that was never closed. The brick walk that led to the house was uneven and grass-grown; while weeds grew unmolested in the hard, dry soil which had been intended for fairer and more fragrant occupants.

Dismal as was the outside of this wretched abode, still more so was the inside. The floor, devoid of carpet, and unacquainted with soap and water, creaked under foot, and in places was badly broken.

The two or three rickety chairs, a rough pine table and crazy bedstead could hardly be dignified with the name of furniture. Some chipped plates and handleless cups were piled in confusion on the table, and had evidently been left there since noon.

A rickety stove, that was propped up on bricks, which did duty for legs, was littered with greasy pots and pans. Ashes strewed the hearth, and the few unbroken lights in the windows were so begrimed with dust as to be of little use, so far as letting in the daylight was concerned.

So much for the dwelling; now for the inmates.

In an old rocking chair sat the mistress of all this misery. In her hands she held a tattered garment, bearing but small semblance to either male or female attire. She had been engaged, apparently, in attempting to draw together some of the many rents into which it had been torn; but whether the task had seemed a hopeless one, or whether her thoughts were far away from her occupation, I cannot say. At any rate, her hands were resting listlessly in her lap, where they had dropped, with the work still unfinished between her fingers.

Aside from the fact that her appearance partook of the general aspect of her surroundings, she was a comely woman, but one upon whose countenance was stamped despair, and, judging from her swollen eye, one also who was the victim of ill-usage.

She was the sole occupant of the room at the time our story opens, but she did not remain so long, for presently the half-open door was pushed back on its unwilling hinge, and a boy of twelve years entered, followed by a little girl of nine. They were both attractive children, notwithstanding the fact that they bore in their appearance and faces the stamp of neglect and scanty fare.

The boy advanced to his mother's side, and throwing himself down on the floor, resting his elbow on her knee and his head upon his hand, burst out impetuously: "Oh, how I wish we could dress decently, and go to school again like other children!"

The mother roused herself from her apathy and looked at him, half curiously, half sadly.

"What now, Clarence? What's the good of wishing for what can't be?" she said, wearily.

"But why can't it be?  It drives me just wild to see
the boys coming from school, and to know that they
have been there learning, while we're just running around
every day; and I'm getting so big too.  Now, there's Tom
and Lizzie Greene; we met them to-day going to school,
looking decent and clean, and, of course, Mr. Tom had
to holler 'ragamuffin' at me; but I didn't give it to him,
did I?"  And the boy chuckled with satisfaction at the
way he had served his tormentor.

"Yes; but, Clarence, I was real sorry for poor Lizzie,
she was so frightened; besides, I like her: she don't call
names, and always speaks to me."

This came from Corinne, Clarence's sister, who had
seated herself on the edge of the ragged bed.

"Come, come, my boy," said Mrs. Burton, taking up
her mending again, in a disheartened way, and beginning
to draw the needle and thread slowly back and forth.
"There's no use talking, and there's no use trying to be
decent when your father is likely to come home drunk at
any time, and knock and beat a body about as he does.
I tell you it's no use talking."  And her voice rang out
sharp and harsh.  "Take the basket," she continued,
after a moment's pause, "and go and get some chips to

start a fire to get some supper, if your father should bring anything home to eat."

Silenced, but not satisfied, the boy obeyed and left the room, followed closely by his sister. He knew that what his mother said was true, and he felt that there was but little benefit to be gained by talking.

Corinne was devotedly fond of her brother, whom she considered a miracle of wisdom; and indeed the lad did have a fund of information about things in general, acquired after the manner usual to observant boys. To this was added an ardent desire to possess an education. Then he was honest and truthful; in fact, he was a boy who might become a useful man; but, as he said to his sister, as he walked slowly along, "he'd no chance."

"Corrie," he exclaimed, suddenly coming to a standstill, and flinging the old basket away from him savagely, "I'm going to run away; so there, now!"

The little girl looked at him in amazement, for a moment, too surprised to say anything. Then the tears gathered in her black eyes, and she said, reproachfully:

"Oh, Clarence! Will you go away and leave me?"

The boy was not proof against the pleading look in the sad little face, for if there was one person in the world whom he really loved, it was his sister. And now, as he looked at her, the fierce hard look slowly died out of his face.

"Now that's just it, Corinne," he said, " if it wasn't for you, I'd go to-morrow; but I do hate to leave you. Never mind, don't cry; maybe something will turn up some day. Here, wipe your eyes on my silk handkerchief."

This had the effect he desired on the little girl, for a smile spread over her face, like sunshine after rain, and she laughed merrily; for the "silk handkerchief" of which her brother spoke was an old bandanna which was so comically dilapidated as to make it a matter of doubt as to whether she would find sufficient handkerchief with which to dry her tears.

While the children were thus engaged with each other a lady approached. The boy and his sister moved aside so that she might pass; but instead of doing this, she came to a stop in front of them.

They looked up into her face in surprise. A very pleasant face it was that they saw, lighted by a pair of very dark and very bright eyes. Clarence knew the face; it was that of a teacher in the school, the very same school that he was so anxious to attend. Yes, he knew her well enough, for he had met her often, and once or twice she had smiled at him, but had never spoken before.

"Your name is Clarence Burton, is it not?" she asked, pleasantly, after surveying the boy from head to foot.

"Yes'm," he answered, looking down at the ground.

"And is the little girl your sister?"

"Yes'm," he said again, "she's Corrie."

"Well, Clarence, why don't you and Corrie come to school?"

"I've nothing fit to come in; neither has Corrie."

"But you would like to come, wouldn't you?"

"Yes, ma'am; it's what I'd like to do more'n anything."

"Won't your mother let you come?"

"Don't know as she'd care, but we ain't going anywhere to be called names, we ain't." And the old hard look came again into the boy's eyes, and he picked up his basket, and was moving away unceremoniously. But it wasn't a part of Miss Gray's plan to have him go yet.

"Clarence," she said, "don't you know that it isn't just polite to do that?"

Something in her voice made Clarence halt, in spite of

himself, although he felt as if he would like very much
to run away as fast as he could.

He looked up again in the lady's face, expecting
to see the "school ma'am" in it, but there was the
same kindly expression in the dark eyes that he had
seen before.

Again he dropped his to the ground, and twisted a
bit of the poor ill-used basket between his uneasy fingers,
but he said not a word.

"Clarence," began Miss Gray again, "I have been
noticing you for a long time, and I have passed by your
home a great many times; and, my poor boy, I know all
about it and I'm so sorry for you." And she reached out
her neatly gloved hand and took the boy's grimy one
and gave it a squeeze.

This was altogether more than Clarence could stand,
especially in his present state of mind, and he snatched
his hand away and hid his face with it. Of course, he
wouldn't have any one think that he was crying—oh, no,
not for a moment; but however that may be, there was a
tremulousness in his voice when he answered Miss Gray's
kind "good-bye." "I'm coming to see your mother soon,
Clarence," she added, with a parting smile at Corinne,

who had done nothing but gaze at the pleasant face of their new acquaintance.

The children watched her for a while after she left them, and then they slowly turned and resumed their interrupted walk. They were going to a new house that was being built, some blocks distant from their home.

Not one word did either of them say until they had reached the building, and were busily engaged in filling their basket with the bits of wood and shavings that had been left by the workmen. When the basket would hold no more they sat down to rest.

"Clarence," said Corinne, looking about her, curiously, "who do you s'pose will live in this house when it's finished?"

"How should I know," returned her brother, rather tartly.

"It's going to be a nice house, Clarence," she went on, without heeding the curtness of the answer to her former question, "and I guess the people that'll live in it will have all sorts of nice things. It must be fine to have all the nice things you want." And the little girl sighed wistfully, as she thought how barren of "nice things" her own poor little life was.

"Don't you fret, Corrie," said her brother, comfortingly; "one of these days you shall have nice things too."

"Where will they come from, Clarence?" asked the child, opening her brown eyes wide.

"Oh, you'll see," was Clarence's answer, given with a wise shake of the head, as he arose to go; and bidding Corinne "come on," he added that the new house was nothing to them, "and never would be." Ah, Clarence, how little we know what the future contains for us!

# CHAPTER II.

## A GRIM VISITOR.

BY the time the children reached home it was dark. No light, however, shone through the dingy windows of the cottage. The boy pushed open the door, and entered, with his sister close behind him.

They found their mother still seated in the old chair, but she was now rocking herself back and forth, her face hidden in her hands, and crying bitterly, but softly.

"What is it, mother?" asked Clarence, anxiously, coming to her side. "What is the matter?"

For answer, his mother pointed to the miserable bed in the corner, upon which was stretched the form of a man.

The boy understood all now. It was no new thing for him to come home and find his mother sobbing over some fresh ill-treatment inflicted upon her by her drink-maddened husband.

For a moment all was still, save for the heavy breathing of the sleeping man. Then the wretched woman

arose, and going noiselessly to the cupboard, took from it
two pieces of bread, and putting them into the hands of
the two children, motioned them to go to bed.  Silently
they obeyed, for upon silence depended their chances of
a quiet night.   Had they been so unfortunate as to waken
the figure upon the bed, a torrent of abuse would have
been theirs : so they were only too glad to creep off to
their beds—Corinne to her pallet on the floor of the
room in which they were, and Clarence to his in the bare
attic.   Then their mother resumed her old position, but
she was quiet now.

Poor little Corinne, too wretched to eat, lay quietly in
her corner, with the great tears chasing each other down
her thin cheeks, until at length she lost sight of her
misery in the sound sleep of childhood.

Clarence, in his hard, comfortless bed, was inwardly
chafing at his lot; his heart was full of bitter, bitter
thoughts against everybody and everything.  It was long
before he slept.

The night wore away and day dawned.  The sunbeams
struggled to peep in at the dirty windows of the cottage,
with but poor success.  They did manage, however, to
flit for an instant across the face of sleeping Corinne.

Perhaps it was this that awakened her; at any rate, waken she did, and, raising herself on her elbow, looked about for her mother. To her surprise, she saw her sitting in the same position in which she had last seen her the evening before. The father was still sleeping on the bed, across which he had thrown himself, hat, boots, and all.

Corinne arose softly, and crept to her mother's side. She had no dressing to do, for she had laid herself down just as she was. Thinking her mother asleep, she stretched out her hand to touch her.

Why did she start back in alarm? Why, indeed? Those dull eyes that stared at her from that stony face plainly told her, child though she was, that her mother was dead. With a wild, frightened cry, she sprang toward the bed where her father lay, and in her terror losing sight of her fear of him, she frantically shook the sleeping man, crying, "Oh, father, father, wake up; do wake up; mother is dead! Oh, what shall I do?"

With an oath her father rolled over, and raising his clenched hand aimed a blow at his child; but Corinne dodged his upraised fist, at the same time continuing her cry.

B

At length the fact slowly dawned upon the man's be-clouded brain that something out of the common had occurred.  He raised himself, and after gazing about him stupidly for a while, arose and walked unsteadily to his wife's side.

Once in front of those wide-open eyes, all apathy dis-appeared, and he seized her by the shoulder and shook her, calling to her to "Wake up!"  But the poor broken-spirited, abused woman was sleeping her last sleep: she would wake no more in this world.

"Oh, father, mother is dead; what made her die?" moaned Corinne.

"I dunno," was the answer.  Then hurriedly bidding her call her brother, the hard-hearted father left the house and hastened away, no one knew whither, leaving the two children all alone with the dead.

Just as the door closed, Clarence came down

"What is the matter, Corrie?" he asked, seeing his sister sobbing so bitterly.

"Oh, Clarence, just look: poor, poor mother is dead."

"Dead?  Mother dead?" ejaculated the boy, in a dazed way, slowly advancing toward the motionless figure.  He lifted one of the nerveless hands, only to let it drop with a shiver as its cold touch met his. For a moment he was silent; then he murmured, half absently, " Yes, dead.  Poor mother!"

"Oh, Clarence!" wailed poor Corrie, pressing close to her brother's side.  The boy put his arm around the trembling little figure.  Poor child! she was so nervous; such a tender little plant!  People used to wonder why she was so different from the rest of the family.  The father, rough, uncouth, and almost always under the influence of liquor.  The mother, careless and unkempt.  Clarence, rugged and impetuous, but thoroughly good-natured.  Corinne both looked and was different from these, and had always been so.

"Clarence, why did mother die?" sobbed the child.

"Why did she die?" repeated the boy, vehemently. "How could she live, battered and beaten, and starved as she was, and by our father too; the one who could have made us all comfortable and happy.  But instead of that he's made us miserable—no, it wasn't him, either; it was that dreadful, dreadful stuff, whisky.  Yes, drink ruined our father, and now it's killed our mother; and nobody cares for us because we're the children of a drunkard.  People don't even want to give me work because of it; and they call me 'old drunken Burton's boy.'"

"Oh, don't, don't talk so; you frighten me," cried Corinne, clinging closer to her brother than ever.

The boy, relieved by having given vent to some of the bitterness that had been pent up in his bosom for so long, now burst into tears, and the brother and sister wept together until they were aroused by a rap on the door.

It was one of the neighbors, who said that their father had stopped at her door and told her that there was something the matter with his "old woman," and had asked her to come and see what it was. Not knowing what had happened, Mrs. Greene had not hurried, having stayed to attend to some of her own household affairs.

Great was her astonishment and deep her indignation when she found how matters stood at the cottage; and she was loud in her denunciations of "that heartless Jim Burton." "No wonder he was moving off so fast, he's likely to be took up for murder. If he ain't killed that poor woman outright, he's done it by inches. But come, chicks, cheer up; don't take on so. Run over to my house, while I fix up here a bit, and tell my Tom you're to have your breakfast." And the kind-hearted woman began turning about to see what she should do first. To her surprise, the boy quietly, but firmly said: "Mrs. Greene, I'd rather not go to your house."

"Why not?" she asked.

"I'd rather not go," he repeated. "I don't want any breakfast."

"Oh, well, of course you needn't go if you don't want to, but you ought to have something to eat. But never mind; I'm going up street a minute or so, and I'll bring you something." And away went Mrs. Greene, spreading, as she went, the news that "Jim Burton's wife had died suddent."

The coroner was notified, and of course there was an inquest, and a verdict rendered that "death was caused by heart trouble," which was true enough, in more senses than one.

But to go back to the children: True to her promise, Mrs. Greene brought with her some breakfast, which she pressed Clarence and Corinne to eat. The worthy woman had attributed the boy's reluctance to visit her house to a backwardness on his part, but in reality it was due to the fact that it was the home of Tom Greene. He was poor, wretchedly poor and forlorn, but he was proud.

He saw in Tom Greene only the boy who delighted in tormenting him, and calling him and his sister names.

Mrs. Greene had also brought with her a tall, spare, hard-featured personage, whom she addressed as "Miss Rachel Penrose," who it seemed was the owner of the old cottage and the ground upon which it stood. A woman of few words was Miss Rachel; one who was "willing to do her duty," as she expressed it, but it was done much after the manner of the Pharisees: her deeds were done to be seen of men. A woman of another stamp was her companion, simple-hearted Mrs. Greene, who was ever ready, from pure sympathy, to lend a hand wherever it was needed; and it was sadly needed here, in this abode of wretchedness and death. She now urged the children to eat, but neither of them was inclined to do so. The boy "wasn't hungry," and his sister was too full of her trouble, so the food was set away untasted.

The coroner had come and gone, so too had the crowd of curious sight-seers; then the task of "cleaning up," which was by no means an easy one, was begun; and Miss Rachel could not forbear remarking in an undertone that it was a mystery to her "how people could be so shiftless," further asserting that to her mind " Mrs. Burton didn't amount to much."

" Ah, Miss Rachel, but you must think of what the poor creature had to put up with! What with Burton's drinkin' and abuse, you wouldn't have much heart to keep things nice if you were starved and knocked about like she was."

Mrs. Greene's defense of the unfortunate woman had but little effect by way of softening her hearer.

" Why didn't she work and keep herself from starving; I'm sure I'd a great sight rather do that and keep myself and children decent, than to give way and just sit down with my hands in my lap and let everything get topsy-turvey."

Miss Rachel's hands were by no means idle while her tongue was busy. Things were getting in pretty good shape under her methodical touch and Mrs. Greene's energetic efforts.

The two forlorn children sat together near the window, in the old rocking chair, too deeply absorbed in their own sorrowful thoughts to heed what was going on around them.

The old bed had been made tidy from good Mrs

Greene's scanty store of bed linen, and the body of the
dead woman, neatly arrayed by the same kind hands,
was lying peacefully upon it.   Nobody knew much about
the Burtons, for they talked to no one.   All that was
known about them was that they had come to the little
cottage one day, with their few belongings, but from
whence no one knew.   Mrs. Burton was neat and respectable looking then; so were her children, who were
quite small.

At first, the place was kept as neat as possible, but
not long; for as the husband and father grew more and
more intemperate, the wife and mother grew disheartened
and careless.   Then, too, the children had been sent to
school, but it had now been a long time since they had
gone.

Clarence was not an idle boy by nature, and he had
tried to get work, and did work when he could get it to
do; but with all his poverty he was very proud, and could
not brook the sneers and taunts of those with whom he
came in contact; so he was not very fortunate in finding
employment.   And just as often as not, when he had
earned a little money, his father had taken it from him
to spend in drink.

Things were in this condition when the grim visitor—"Death"—stepped in and removed the mother.

She had lived a hopeless life, and no one knew otherwise than that she had died a hopeless death. She had gone without a word, and none save God knew aught of her last moments.

# CHAPTER III.

## FRIENDS.

THE long night passed slowly away in the little cottage. Mrs. Greene, the only person, except Miss Rachel Penrose, who had come near the children since their bereavement, for anything more than curiosity, stayed with them. They had both slept a little, but the night had seemed very dreary, and they were glad when morning dawned. Their mother was to be buried that day by the town, for their father had gone away, no one knew where. He had not been seen since he left the cottage the morning before, save by Mrs. Greene, with whom he had exchanged a few words, asking her to go over and see what ailed his wife.

About six o'clock, the kind neighbor left them for a while, to go to her home in order to prepare breakfast for her family. Thinking that Clarence and Corinne would be more likely to eat something if Lizzie carried it to them, she accordingly sent the little girl over with some coffee and toast. She thought rightly, for the shy ways and sympathizing words of the child won the brother and sister from their lonely sorrow, and she succeeded in coaxing them to eat a little of the toast and drink the coffee.

Mrs. Greene entered while the three sat quietly talking together. She brought with her a suit of clothes for Clarence and a dress for Corinne, so that they might follow their mother to her grave, looking at least respectable. The clothes, she thought, would do nicely, for Tom and Clarence were about the same size, and Lizzie was very little larger than Corinne.

The two little girls parted reluctantly, but were pleased when they were told that Corinne should come and stay with Lizzie after the funeral. As Lizzie Greene passed out at the gate, she met Miss Gray just going in. Remembering her promise to Clarence, she had determined to stop at the cottage, on her way to school, and have a talk with Mrs. Burton. With a smile to Lizzie, she walked up the uneven path and tapped lightly on the door. It was not until she had rapped that she noticed the crape upon it.

Clarence, who from the window had caught a glimpse of his new friend, hastened to meet her. All unprepared

for the sad scene that met her gaze, she exclaimed:
"Why, Clarence! What does this mean?"

"Mother died night before last, ma'am," explained
the boy, as steadily as he could, while Corinne only
sobbed.

"Yes, miss," volunteered Mrs. Greene, coming forward;
"she died quite suddenly. Nobody knows how, nor just
when."

"Poor children!" murmured Miss Gray. Then addressing the friendly neighbor, she asked: "Where is
her husband?"

"That's what none of us can tell, miss. He took himself off as soon as it happened."

"And left these children here all alone?"

"That's what he did, miss."

"Poor things!" And the visitor sat down, and draw-
ing the weeping Corinne to her, gently soothed her, while
the boy told all he knew of the sad story.

The young school teacher stayed as long as she could
with the lonely children, and when she left at last it
seemed to them as if she had taken a part of the sunshine
with her. Miss Gray was full of sympathy for her little
friends, and as she walked along her thoughts were busy

trying to devise some way in which to help them. They
were in her thoughts all day, and when school was over,
and she turned her steps homeward, she was still thinking of them. It was a beautiful afternoon in June. The
sun was shining brightly upon the flowers in the tasteful
gardens in front of the pretty homes that lined the quiet
streets through which she passed. Here and there, a
gay butterfly fluttered, or a busy bee flitted from blossom
to blossom.

"The world seems very lovely and peaceful this
afternoon," thought the young girl, as she paused
before the gate of her own little home. She lifted the
latch and walked slowly up the neatly kept walk to the
house.

"The home of Helen Gray was a small but picturesque
white cottage, over whose porch clambered roses and
honeysuckle, and in whose garden bloomed many a bright
blossom. Inside, the little house was as neat, cool, and
cosy as the hands of Mary, Helen's younger sister, could
make it. Mary was an invalid. She had been frail and
sickly from a little child. She was therefore unable to
mingle with the busy world, but did her very best to
make home pleasant for her beloved sister. Although

she was not given to repining,—her disposition was altogether too sweet and gentle for that,—she could not help fretting sometimes because she could not go out and work, and earn money too. But Helen would always say: "No, no, dear. Let me do the going, and you the staying. I couldn't do both, you know." And then she would laugh merrily, but would add, more soberly: "What would I do if I had no Mary to keep house for me, and to talk to me when I come home? You are a very important personage, Miss Mary, and you must endure your importance as best you can."

The two sisters lived all alone, the elder supporting both by her teaching. They were orphans, and were strongly attached to each other.

On this afternoon, Mary was sitting by the open window sewing, ever and anon looking up to admire the bright picture without, and to enjoy the perfume of the flowers, as the soft breeze wafted it to her. A smile stole over her thin face as she saw her sister approaching. An answering smile lit up the features of Helen as she came to the invalid's side, and stooped and kissed the upturned lips. Then removing her hat, she seated herself in a low rocking chair, exclaiming: "How sweet and cool you have made it in here, Mary! I declare it *is* pleasant to come home."

"I'm very glad you think so, dear," was the pleased reply.

"It seems more pleasant than ever to me to-day, after what I've seen."

"Why, where have you been?"

"I went to see those poor children I was telling you about the other day—and what do you think? Their mother died suddenly the night before last. They are wretchedly poor. I never was so shocked in my life."

"Poor, poor children!" said Mary, pityingly.

"And that's not all," continued her sister. "Their father went off and left them as soon as he found out about the mother."

"Oh, Helen, how sad! Can't we do something for them?"

"That's just what I've been puzzling my brain to find out," was the answer.

"Who will bury the poor woman?"

"The town, of course. They have no friends—at least, nobody seems to know anything about them."

"Poor things!" again said Mary.

"I'm going to help you sew some now, Mary." And Helen slipped on her thimble, threaded a needle, and began to stitch away industriously.

For some minutes the sisters worked on in silence, then Mary looked up and said, softly, her sweet smile lighting up the wan face: "'And the King shall answer and say unto them: Verily I say unto you, inasmuch as ye have done it unto one of the least of these my brethren, ye have done it unto me.' Sister, we must help those children."

"That's easily said, Mary dear, but how are we to do it? Oh, here comes Dr. Barrett! Now suppose we ask him about the boy? Maybe he can do something for him. We'll do it!" And the young girl arose and went to the door to welcome the genial-faced old gentleman, who had alighted from his buggy and was now coming up the walk.

Dr. Barrett was an old friend of the sisters. He had been the family physician ever since the girls could remember. He had always been their friend, and since the death of their parents seemed more like a father to them. He had attended Mary from her first illness, and insisted on coming every once in a while to see her, even when she was in her usual health. She was never really well. The girls were always glad to see his buggy stop before their gate.

"Well, how are we to-day?" was his cheery greeting, as he put his head in at the door.

"No; I can't come in. I've a new horse, and he won't stand long—Whoa, there, Ned! Can't you wait a minute?" he called to the restless animal, which, finding itself free, was not slow to take advantage of his liberty, perhaps thinking it a good time to go for a stroll on his own account. He was interrupted, however, in time to prevent any such undesirable proceeding.

"I must get a boy. That horse won't stand unless he has some one to hold him," panted the doctor, as he again ascended the steps, having given Mr. Ned in charge of a small lad.

"A boy, did you say, Dr. Barrett?" cried Helen, while Mary listened attentively.

"Yes, 'a boy.' Is there anything wonderful about that?" returned the doctor.

"Well, yes," retorted Helen, mischievously. "There is something wonderful about it."

"Indeed? I'd like to know what it is, then."

c

"There's something both wonderful and fortunate about your wanting a boy just now. We have one all ready for you, and you *must* take him, you know."

"Is there a 'must' about it too?"

"Yes, indeed; and a penalty to pay if you disobey."

"What will the penalty be, pray?"

"Why, we shan't like you any more."

"Speak for yourself, Helen," put in Mary, laughing.

"Now you keep out of this, Mary, and let me manage things," said Helen, playfully shaking her finger at her sister. Then turning again to the doctor, she asked, with mock gravity: "Do you accept the conditions, sir?"

"I do," answered he, in the same tone.

"So you promise to take the boy we have for you?"

"I promise, most solemnly, to take the boy, if he suits me; and not to, if he doesn't."

"Now you are too bad, Dr. Barrett," cried Helen. "But I shall send him to your office, just the same."

"All right; send him up," was the reply. Then, dropping his jesting tone, he said: "I guess he'll do. If you are so anxious about the matter, I'll try him for a while."

"Oh, I'm pretty sure he will suit you. He seems to be such a steady, independent sort of boy." And then she told the old gentleman the story we already know, to which he listened with interest, expressing sympathy and promising to do what he could for Clarence, if he proved worthy.

After a pleasant little chat, the good doctor arose to go, telling Helen to "be sure and send the boy up as soon as possible." This she was more than willing to promise.

"I consider that a special providence, Mary," she said, when they were once more alone. "To think that Dr. Barrett should want a boy at this time!"

"'He shall give thee the desires of thine heart,'" repeated her sister, reverently.

Helen smiled. "It seems to me that you have a text for everything. But now it's about time for tea." And she began putting away her sewing.

It was true, as her sister had said. Mary had a verse, or part of a verse, to fit in almost everywhere. The invalid loved her Bible. It was her constant companion, and she knew it well.

# CHAPTER IV.

### PROVIDED FOR.

CLARENCE was quite as determined that he would not wear Tom Greene's clothes to his mother's funeral as he had been that he would not go to Tom Greene's home the day before; so, leaving his sister and Mrs. Greene together, he climbed up to his attic, and having succeeded in finding materials, proceeded to draw together, as best he could, the rents in the garments his poor mother had been attempting to mend on the last sad day of her life. The articles consisted of a jacket and trousers; and he was working away industriously, if not skillfully, when Corinne, who had missed him, stole quietly upon him.

"Whatever are you doing, Clarence?" she asked.

"Oh, nothing much," he answered; "only fixing these things to put on."

"But you won't need them, Clarence. Mrs. Greene has brought a nice suit of her Tom's for you to wear. Why, you know that!"

"Yes, I know it well enough. I shan't wear it, though."

"Not wear the clothes Mrs. Greene brought!"

"No; I'd rather wear the worst kind of rags than put on Tom Greene's things and have him throw it in my face afterward."

"Oh, but, Clarence, Mrs. Greene will be angry! And she has been so good to us! I am to wear a dress of Lizzie's."

"Oh, it's all right about you; they wouldn't bother you. Just let me do as I want to about this, Corrie, there's a good girl. I'll make it all right with Mrs. Greene. She needn't know why I don't want to wear the clothes she brought. Run away down, now, won't you?"

Corrie did as she was told; and her brother, finishing his mending, put on the garments and went down.

"Why, Clarence, I thought you were putting on the suit I brought for you. Hurry, now, and get it on," cried Mrs. Greene.

"I'd rather wear these things, Mrs. Greene, please," stammered the boy.

"Why, what on earth——" began the puzzled woman

impatiently. But she was interrupted by a knock on
the door.

There was no further time to spend in talking, for the
hearse was waiting for its burden. The mother, in her
rough coffin, was placed within, and the two children
followed it to the burial place, where a short service was
read; and then the earth was thrown in upon all that
was mortal that remained of their parent. The two
children had cried so much that they could do nothing
now but stand and look on in a dazed sort of way. When
all was over they turned sadly and walked away.

Mrs. Greene was waiting for them at the door of the
little cottage. She had determined not to notice any
further the boy's refusal to wear the clothes. She told
the children that she was waiting to take them home
with her to pass the night. To her astonishment, Clarence said, quietly :

"You have been very kind to us, Mrs. Greene, and
we're very thankful to you for all you have done for us;
but, if you please, ma'am, I am going to stay here
to-night. Corrie can do as she likes; she can go if she
wants to."

"No, no, Clarence; I'll stay with you," whispered his

sister, although the vision of Mrs. Greene's cozy, neat rooms was a great deal more inviting than the dingy, dreary cottage. But she was unwilling to leave her brother alone. He was all she had to look up to, and she wanted to be near him.

"Well, Clarence Burton," said Mrs. Greene, when she had recovered enough to say anything, "I didn't think you were such an ungrateful, headstrong boy. But there; that's all one has a right to expect from such people." And she walked away with an angry air.

"Oh, Clarence! I thought she would be angry," said Corinne, regretfully.

"Well, I can't help it," answered her brother. "Of course, I'm thankful for what she has done; but that doesn't make me want to go to her house. I couldn't go there, and that's all about it." He turned and entered the house, and Corinne followed.

The night seemed very long and dreary, especially to the little girl, who was a timid, nervous child; and daylight was a welcome sight. Good Mrs. Greene, although she was angry at the boy's persistent refusal to come to her home, could not bring herself to forget the forlorn children entirely; so she sent Lizzie over with some breakfast, which they were glad to receive, and for which they thanked her warmly.

Early that morning, their friend, Miss Gray, came to deliver her message to Clarence, who received it with real pleasure. Having done this, she was about to tell Corinne to get ready to go home with her for the day, when Miss Rachel Penrose unceremoniously entered.

As I have already said, Miss Rachel was the owner of the wretched old cottage; and she had come to tell the children that it would be no longer their home. When she heard that the boy had been offered a situation, she nodded her head approvingly, and said that, "seein' as the boy's provided for, I guess I'll take the girl. She's likely to be of service to run errands and wash dishes and such."

And so it was settled, and the cottage was closed. Corinne went to her new home with Miss Rachel, and Clarence went with Miss Gray, who was to show him the way to Dr. Barrett's office. He found that good gentleman just getting ready to go out.

"Oh, so you're 'the boy,' are you?" he said, adjusting his gold-rimmed spectacles to get a better view of him. "What is your name?"

"Clarence Burton, sir."

"Clarence, is it, eh? Well, that's a good name. Now, Clarence, I've got to go out for a while. Just turn about in here, and rub things up generally; for everything is at sixes and sevens, as the saying goes. I had a good smart boy, but he was taken sick and compelled to go home, and I haven't been able to find another to suit me, until I heard about you."

Clarence, much pleased at his hearty reception, promised to do his best to please the good doctor.

After giving directions as to how he wanted things "rubbed up," and charging him to be careful, he went out, leaving the boy feeling very strange and queer. He set to work, however—clumsily enough, to be sure, at first, but with the determination to do his best to give satisfaction.

Meanwhile, Corinne had gone with Miss Penrose. "Miss Rachel Penrose, Seamstress," was the announcement the plate on her door made to the passers-by. Miss Rachel was a spinster who supported herself by her needle. Not that she was wholly dependent upon it for a living; for besides owning the house in which she lived and the cottage in which the Burtons had lived, she had a snug sum of money in the savings bank. As she was a good seamstress, she had a large run of custom and was well paid for her work.

But Miss Rachel was stingy. "Saving" was her besetting sin. Now the habit of saving, when exercised wisely and properly, is a virtue; but when saving means depriving one's self, and others, of the actual necessities of life, in order to lay away money for the sake of simply *possessing*, then it becomes a vice.

It had become so with Miss Rachel. Every cent she spent was parted with as though it were a drop of blood, without which she could not possibly survive. She counted her coals, she counted the potatoes, she meted out everything with the smallest measurement possible. A bright fire, in her opinion, was a waste, and enough to eat entirely unnecessary.

Such was the woman with whom our little friend Corinne had found a home. The child had led an idle, useless life. Her mother had made no effort whatever to train her in any way. Indeed, she had paid but little attention to her children since their earliest years. She had given way altogether to despondency, and had lost all energy and ambition, doing hardly anything, save to sit and brood bitterly and rebelliously over the fate that had shut out from her the light of happiness. Had Mrs. Burton been a Christian she would not have done so, but would have sought to rear her boy and girl properly, and would have striven to accept her lot at least cheerfully. But she was not a Christian, and, therefore, lived as one without hope. She had been born and reared in the country, but had been early deprived of her parents. She had been cared for by strangers, and had grown to be a giddy, thoughtless girl. She had met and formed the acquaintance of James Burton; and although she well knew that he was given to hard drinking, she married him. There had been friendly people who had advised her to do otherwise, and had warned her of the dangers before her; but she was headstrong, and so chose her own way and found it full of thorns. She had thought she knew best, and cherished many bright hopes for a happy future. But alas! like the man in the Lord's sermon, she had built upon the sand. And the rain descended, and the floods came, and the winds blew, and beat upon her house; and it fell, and great was the fall of it.

When she could, she would not hear; and when she

saw her bright prospects slipping from her she had
nothing to cling to—no hope in this world nor in the
world to come.   Was it any wonder, then, that she had
drifted into the wretched creature she became?  With
their two little children, the unhappy couple left their
country home and came to N—— to live in the old
cottage, which was only fit to be torn down.   For this
they paid but little, but more than the place was worth;
its owner saw to that.   Proud and mortified, Mrs. Burton
had shut herself up, alone with her wretchedness, and
had repelled all attempts on the part of her neighbors
to befriend her.   To pay the bit of house rent was now
pretty much the extent of James Burton's provision for
his family; and so it was but a short while before the
abused and despondent wife lost all care as to whether
things were kept in order or not.   The children went to
school as long as their clothes lasted; and, be it said to
her credit, their mother did mend and fix over their
scanty wardrobe as long as it could be done, and some
of the hottest battles between the wretched pair were
fought that she might obtain decent clothing for them.
But she wearied of the struggle at last, and the garments
had become so worn that they were no longer fit to wear

to school, especially as the more favored but cruelly thoughtless children had taken advantage of this to nickname the brother and sister " ragamuffins " ; and so they went to school no more. Clarence did odd jobs whenever he could get them to do, and but for this the lot of his mother and Corinne would have been even harder than it was.

These were the surroundings amid which Corinne Burton had passed her young life. It is but natural to conclude that it was a sudden change from such a home as I have already described to one where everything was as prim and orderly as its prim mistress.

Miss Rachel Penrose had had a girl to do her housework, but she had been taken ill, and had gone to her home just previous to the death of Mrs. Burton. It was on the day when Miss Rachel had gone to the cottage at the request of Mrs. Greene, that she conceived the idea of supplying the place of her former maid-of-all-work with the homeless little Corinne, persuading herself into the belief that she was very benevolent and charitable to take a motherless child and provide her with a home and food, which she would pay for by the help she would render in her home.

# CHAPTER V.

## CORINNE'S NEW HOME.

A MONTH had elapsed since Corinne first entered her new home. It was now July. One warm morning, Miss Rachel, seated in her accustomed place, sewing, was dividing her attention between her work and the little girl, who was washing and polishing the front windows. She had rubbed the panes again and again, until her arms ached, and still Miss Rachel declared that they were not fit to look at; "but you can't stand there rubbing all day, so they'll have to do, I 'spose. Go, now, and scrub that kitchen floor, and mind, if it don't suit me when you're done, I'll make you do it over till it does; and don't be long about it, either."

The small tired arms and hands hastened to get pail and brush, and to scrub, scrub, scrub, only to be told that the floor looked "as bad as before." Poor child! it had been this way ever since the day she came there from the cottage, and it seemed to her that, hard as her lot had been before, it was doubly so now. Nothing but hard work from morning until night.   Not a moment of the day which she could call her own, her hard task mistress begrudging her the time spent in eating the meagre food she allowed her; and sometimes even the privilege of eating at all was on the slightest pretext denied her.   As a general thing, the child arose from her bed hungry, and retired to it again hungry when the day was over.   She cried herself to sleep nearly every night, partly from weariness, partly from grief.

If Miss Rachel had only spoken a kind word to her once in a while, she thought she would not have minded so much about the rest; but the hard features of the seamstress had no smiles for the sad-faced little Corinne, and the thin lips voiced no words for her, more pleasant than an order to do something, or a complaint that some other thing had not been satisfactorily done.   It was no wonder, then, that the child grew thinner than ever, as the weary days dragged themselves by.

Clarence had been to see her once one day, while Miss Rachel was out.   The doctor could not spare him often, he said.   He looked well and happy, and Corinne had been so glad to see him that she had disliked to mar the pleasure of his visit with complaints.   Young as she was, she felt that nothing could be done about the matter, so she had given herself up to the enjoyment of the moment.

This visit had cheered the little girl very much, and her heart felt lighter that night as she lay down to rest, and she thought of her brother a long time before she fell asleep. He had talked to her about his situation and the kindness of his employer, and had confided to her his plans, which seemed to her simple mind nothing short of wonderful; and the thought of these plans made her forget, for the time being, that for her the old, dreary, uneventful life would commence again with the morning light.

Clarence had drawn the conclusion, from the very tidy appearance of the house, that his sister was fortunate in having such a home, especially since Corinne had made no complaints, and had evaded his question as to whether she liked to live there.

The boy himself was doing well. Naturally quick, and scrupulously honest and truthful, he had proved very useful to the good doctor. He felt that he had now " the chance," as he expressed it, for which he had wished so long; and he had fully made up his mind to improve it to the utmost.

The doctor, seeing that the boy was ambitious to make something of himself, sympathized with him and gave him some old school books, which he found stowed away in a corner of his bookcase. These books the boy studied carefully during his leisure moments, with occasionally a little help from the doctor. He had told Corinne that he meant to make a man of himself, and also that his fixed determination was to make a home for her; and when he had pictured to her that home, and the many comforts it was to contain, she had been too happy to do anything but clasp her hands and say, "Oh, Clarence!"

These were the plans that brightened the hours of the night after her brother's visit. Indeed, the memory of that visit and the vision of the home her brother was to make for them was the subject of her thoughts for days afterward.

She did not know it, but there was another glimmer of light coming into her dull life. It came after this fashion: Her friend, Miss Gray, had been absent during the summer holidays with her sister. They had been to pay a visit to one of their father's relatives who lived in the country, several hours' ride from N——.

It was the latter part of August when they returned.

D

One of the first things Helen Gray did was to call on Miss Rachel Penrose, ostensibly to have a chat, but in reality to see how Corinne was getting along. The child was out at the time, so she seated herself and began talking to Miss Rachel, who, having always on hand an abundance of topics upon which to talk, was by no means averse to having a little conversation. In answer to her queries, she told her caller all that had happened during her absence; not that there had been any very important happenings, but such as there had been were made the most of.

Her visitor listened apparently much interested, but inwardly wishing that Corinne would come. At length, just as she was about to go, the child came in, looking hot and tired, and so thin and wretched that Helen could scarcely repress an exclamation of pity. But feeling that the keen gray eyes of the seamstress were looking at her sharply, and fearing that she might make trouble for the little girl, she checked herself, and simply said: "Why, Corinne, how do you do?"

Corinne, overjoyed at sight of the kind familiar face, had noticed the fleeting expression of sympathy in it. She was a little disappointed at the indifferent tone of

Clarence and Corinne

Miss Gray's voice when she spoke to her. She tried, however, to smile and answer cheerfully, as she knew Miss Rachel desired her to do; but it was a very pitiful smile, and she was only too glad to hurry away before her stern guardian should notice the quivering lip and gathering teardrops.

Helen had seen enough to convince her that the poor motherless child was unhappy and oppressed. She soon rose to go, saying as she did so, as carelessly as she could: "Miss Rachel, I would like it if you would let Corinne come to see me next Sunday afternoon. Does she go to Sunday-school?"

"No," was the answer, "she's no time to go; besides, what would the likes of her want there? It would just put notions in her head, and she'd be getting above her place."

"But ——," gently remonstrated Miss Gray, startled out of her caution. "But you are a church member yourself, and surely you would not want the child grow up like a heathen?"

"I'd wish you to know, miss, that I know what's my duty, and what's not, too," retorted Miss Rachel; adding "and I need none of your telling."

"I beg your pardon, Miss Penrose," Helen hastened to say, feeling that she had injured her own cause. "I beg your pardon! Of course, you know your duty; I did not mean to say you did not; but won't you let Corinne come to see my sister some Sunday afternoons? She would like so much to have her to teach. You know she is an invalid, and can't go out much, and she does long so to have a class in the Sunday-school. It would please her to have Corinne. You will let her come, won't you?"

"Well," said Miss Rachel, slowly, somewhat mollified by the coaxing tones, "well, I can't promise for often, but maybe she can come sometimes, seeing it's you as wants her."

"Thank you," said Helen, congratulating herself upon gaining her point so easily. "May she come next Sunday?"

"I'll see about it; maybe so," was the reply. And the visitor took her leave.

When Helen reached home, she found her sister lying upon the sofa, with her eyes closed. Thinking her asleep, she stole softly to her side, and stood looking down into the face so sadly pinched and drawn by sickness and pain, the face so dear to her; and the thought that it looked thinner than ever caused her heart to beat, with the dread that one day she might miss from her side the only being left upon earth whom she could claim as her own. But only for an instant did she allow this thought to tarry; stooping, she lightly kissed the brow of the supposed sleeper. As she did so, the dark eyes unclosed, and Mary looked up into her face with her sweet smile, and said: "Did you think I was asleep?"

"Why, of course I did, you naughty child," returned her sister, pretending to be displeased. "What do you mean by shamming in that way?"

"I wasn't shamming—at least, I didn't mean to be."

"What were you doing then? You said you were not asleep," said Helen, curiously.

"I was just thinking, as I do lots of times when I am all alone."

"Thinking of what, dear?"

"Oh, of different things. Just then I was wondering if I had a mission, and what it was."

"Well, that's easily enough answered," said Helen. "Your mission is to be my sweet little sister and companion; isn't that mission enough for you?"

"No, Helen, I don't think it is; it's almost too pleasant to be considered so; besides, if there's any mission about it, it belongs to you. There is little I can do for you, and you do all for me. I am not necessary to you, but you are to me."

"Now, there's just where you are wrong, my dear; you are altogether and entirely necessary to me. But if it will please you better, my mission is to care for you, and yours to care for me; will that do?"

"Yes, that will do very well, so far as it goes."

"'So far as it goes'; you ungrateful girl! What do you mean?"

"Why, I mean that I'd like to do something for some one else besides you. I want to feel that I am doing good to somebody."

"Oh, if that's all, I think your wish can be gratified."

Helen had left her sister's side during this conversation, and had busied herself with laying the table for the evening meal. Having set the tea to draw, she came and sat down near Mary's sofa, and taking some sewing from the little workstand beside her, began to stitch away.

"How can my wish be gratified?" asked the invalid,

watching the deft fingers of her sister with her large liquid eyes.

"Just this way," was the reply: "That poor child, Corinne Burton—you remember Corinne, don't you, whose mother died just a little while before we went to the country?"

"Oh, yes," answered Mary. "And whose father went off and left her and her brother all alone. I remember Corinne. What about her?"

"Well, she went to live with that prim Miss Rachel Penrose, the seamstress. I was so glad, because being apparently a very exemplary woman, I was quite sure she would have a good home."

"Well, didn't she?" queried Mary, anxiously.

"The home is good enough," said Helen, "but she isn't treated well."

"How do you know?"

"Because I went to see her to-day, and she looks very thin and weak; as if she were overworked. Miss Penrose spoke so crossly to her too; in fact, the child looks more miserable than she did when she was living at home in that wretched old shanty."

"Oh, Helen!" exclaimed Mary. "How sorry I am

for her! But what can you do, and what has she to do
with what we were talking about just now?"

"A great deal. I've coaxed Miss Penrose to let her
come here Sunday afternoons—partly that Corinne may
have a pleasant change, and partly because I thought
you would like to give her some Bible lessons."

"Yes, indeed, Helen dear; that's just what I should
like of all things."

"I thought you would; and you can do the poor child
ever so much good. But come, Mary, you must have
your tea." And rising, she placed her arm about her
sister's waist and tenderly led her to her seat at the
table.

# CHAPTER VI.

### A DISAPPOINTMENT.

CORINNE awoke on the Sunday morning following
Miss Gray's visit with a new and strange sensation.
This was the day she was to go, for the first time, to the
home of the kind young lady whose smiling face was
seldom out of her mind now. With a light heart she
arose, and began her usual tasks with unusual cheerful-
ness, which did not fail to make itself apparent to Miss
Rachel, who of course guessed what it meant.

Miss Rachel was pharisaical in her make-up, and
always made a great show of piety. Especially did she
do so on Sundays. She invariably attended church in the
morning, rain or shine, snow or blow. She considered
when she had done this that her duty was done, so far as
church was concerned. That Corinne should go sometimes never suggested itself to her as at all necessary.
She was careful to leave sufficient work to last the child
until she came home, and woe to her if it was not done.

In the afternoon, after everything was cleared up, she

made the child, who had just begun to read a little, take the Bible and read aloud a chapter. Not one that contained anything she could understand, but such as the twenty-eighth or twenty-ninth of Numbers, all about sacrifices, etc. The majority of the words Corinne was obliged to spell, and altogether it was very dull, dry, hard work, and made her eyes and head ache. As she was never allowed to have the Bible any other day except Sunday, she knew nothing of its contents save the part which was given her to read on that day. Miss Rachel considered that she was acting the part of a Christian guardian in making the child plod through such verses as: "And one goat, for a sin-offering; beside the continual burnt-offering; and his meat-offering, and his drink-offering." What it all meant Corinne had not the slightest idea, and indeed I am not at all sure that Miss Rachel knew much more about it than did she. The beautiful stories of "Joseph," "Daniel," "Samuel," and others were unknown to the little girl, and the precious truths of the New Testament—the history of the birth, life, and death of the dear Saviour—were all hidden treasures of which she was entirely ignorant.

In one respect, however, Sundays were a relief from

week days, and that was that she was sent to bed immediately after tea. But it was all very dull and lonely, for she was never allowed to go out except on errands.

Was it strange, then, that the prospect of a change of any kind should delight her? Willingly and swiftly did Corinne perform her tasks while Miss Rachel was at church, taking especial care to do them just as well as she could. The dinner, which differed but little from the week-day meal, was all ready and on the table when she came home. When it was over, and the dishes cleared away, as Miss Rachel had said nothing about it, she ventured to ask if she might "go to Miss Gray's now." She had had no thought but that the partial promise would be fulfilled, but to her dismay Miss Rachel told her coldly that she could not go, as she was going out herself, and she did not wish the house left with no one in it.

Corinne was bitterly disappointed. She turned quickly away to hide the hot tears that forced themselves from her eyes, and which she dared not let fall in her guardian's presence. They fell thick and fast, however, when the front door closed upon her. Corinne cried for a while as if her heart would break, and the tears were

still falling when she was startled by a rap on the door.
Thinking it was Miss Rachel who had changed her mind
about going out, and had returned, she hurriedly dried
her eyes before opening the door.   To her surprise and
delight, she found that it was her brother.

"Oh, Clarence!" she cried.

"Hello, Corrie!" returned he.

"I'm so glad you've come."

"So am I.   But what's the matter?   You've been
crying.   Has anybody hurt you?"

"No," answered Corinne, hesitatingly.   She disliked
to worry her brother with her troubles when she knew
he could do her no good.

"Well, what were you crying about?" persisted Clarence, with an air that said plainly, "I mean to know, so
you might as well hurry up and tell."

So Corinne told him the story of her disappointment.

"The mean old thing!" exclaimed Clarence, angrily.

"Never mind about it now, Clarence.   It's all right
since you're here.   I'd have missed seeing you if I had
gone."

"But it *was* mean in her, and I'd like to tell her so,"
still fumed the boy.

"Oh, well, that wouldn't do any good, and would make her all the harder on me. Come, now, don't let's talk any more about that. Tell me something about yourself." And she seated herself beside him.

"Well, Corrie," began Clarence, twisting about uncomfortably, "here's another rub. I most hate to tell you."

"What is it? Tell me. I guess I'll not mind."

"Well, I hope you won't; but I going to L—— next week," said the boy, abruptly, hurrying to get the unpleasant task over.

"Going to L—— next week?" repeated Corinne, as if she did not know what the words meant. "Oh, Clarence! going to leave me?" she cried, as she began to realize their meaning.

"Now, see here, Corrie," her brother hastened to say, consolingly, "I'm going away to earn money to make that home we were talking about when I was here last time." And Clarence gently patted his sister's head, which she had laid on his shoulder.

"Why, ain't you making money where you are?" sobbed Corinne,

"Oh, I don't get much besides my clothes and board at the doctor's. He's kind to me, to be sure, and gives

me a little extra change once in a while. I've been
saving up, and I've got a little more than enough to take
me to L——, where I am sure I can get a place in a
store of some kind. I'd like that kind of work ever so
much better; and then, you know, I'm sure to make more
money," he said, emphasizing the argument which he
thought most likely to recommend itself to his sister.
"I'm awful sorry that you've got such a hard one to live
with," he continued, "but don't you mind; it'll all come
out right one of these days. I'll go by Miss Gray's as I
go home, and tell her all about it. Maybe she can get
Miss Rachel to let you come next Sunday."

"Yes, do, Clarence," said Corinne, drying her eyes,
and feeling a little comforted as she listened while Clarence drew bright pictures of what was to be in the future.

When her brother rose to go, she could not help the
tears coming again, as she thought how soon he was to
leave her.

"Don't fret so, Corrie," said he. "It's the best thing
I can do, and you'll believe so when you hear that I've
a good place and am saving money, for I mean to save
every cent I can. It won't be long, so don't take on so
about my going. I'll write to you as soon as I get some-

thing to do, and then I'll write often afterward, and you'll know just how I'm getting along. That'll be nice, won't it, Corrie ?' "

" Yes," answered the little girl, smiling faintly through her tears. " Can you write a letter, Clarence ?" she asked, admiringly.

"Oh, of course, I can't write so very well, but I can write some—you know I could before I left school, and I've been practicing a good bit lately. Dr. Barrett has helped me some too, when he wasn't busy. He's heard me read and spell. I mean to go to night school when I get settled. Now, good-bye, Corrie ; I must go. I'll come in again before I go." And with another "good-bye," Clarence was gone.

It was not so very long after he left, that another tap at the door announced the fact that Miss Rachel had returned. Poor Corinne had entirely forgotten, so busy had she been with her brother, that she should have been getting tea ready ; and now, as Miss Rachel glanced in surprise around the room, she remembered it for the first time.

" Well, miss, what have you been doing ever since I've been gone not to have tea ready ?"

Corinne stammered that Clarence had been there, and she had been talking to him, and had forgotten that it was nearly tea time.

"Very well," was the sharp response; "that shows that *you* don't stand in need of your supper very badly, so you can go to bed. I'll get my own."

Poor Corinne went silently up stairs to her bare little room, and throwing herself upon the bed sobbed violently. She thought that surely there could not live a more unhappy little girl than herself. After she had cried until it seemed as if she could cry no more, she sat up on the bed, dried her swollen eyes, and looked listlessly about the room.

There was nothing in it but her bed and an old broken stand. Indeed, it was too small to hold anything else. There was an old empty closet in one corner, the door of which had been missing for many years. Upon a shelf at the top the wandering eyes of Corinne spied something small and brown. It looked like a book, and the child, being lonely, and glad of anything for a change, determined to get it, if for nothing else than to divert her attention from the hunger that was making her feel almost sick.

She pulled the old stand across the floor as carefully and noiselessly as she could for fear of attracting the attention of the occupant of the room below. Mounting the rickety thing, she reached up and took down the old book and wiped the thick coating of dust from its dingy cover. Clambering down from the stand, and replacing it, she seated herself again on the side of the bed and opened the antiquated volume. It was still daylight, so that she could see that the book was a Bible. At first she was disappointed, the sight of the yellow pages bringing vividly to her mind the Sunday afternoon readings. But she was so lonely that even these would help pass away some of the time, so she went as near the window as she could get. It was too high up for her to reach its sill without the aid of the old stand, which she was afraid to attempt to move again. So she stood beneath the window, in order to see clearly, and opened the book again. This time she opened it at the New Testament. Glancing down the page for something that looked as if she could understand it, her eye caught the words: "Casting all your care upon him; for he careth for you."

Again and again, she slowly and carefully spelt it out, until the words were fixed in her mind. What comfort-

E

# CHAPTER VII.

## CORINNE'S VISIT.

CLARENCE, mindful of his promise to Corinne, stopped on his way home, to explain to Miss Gray why she had not come that afternoon.

The sisters were sorry, particularly on the little girl's account; for they knew that she must have been very much disappointed at not being allowed to come.

They were sorry too to hear that Clarence was going to leave N———. Still they agreed with him, when he told them of his hopes and aspirations, that it would be best. They promised him that they would see after his sister, and assured him that she should be placed in another home as soon as one could be procured, and Miss Rachel could be induced to give her up.

Helen secretly anticipated trouble in getting the consent of the exacting woman to any such proceeding; for she well knew that Corinne was the means of saving her self-constituted guardian no small sum, since she paid her no wages. The scanty food and poor clothing the child received was but little reward for the quantity of labor required of her.

But Helen said nothing of her thoughts to the others; for she knew that they would worry the poor boy, who was so bent on making a way in the world for himself and his beloved sister. His heart was much lighter when he resumed his walk homeward; and many were the castles in the air he built as he walked.

Helen and Mary Gray sat and talked long after he had gone, but could arrive at no solution of the perplexing problem as to how and where a home was to be found for their little protégé. They would have taken her into their own; but the salary Helen received for her teaching was barely sufficient to provide for the wants of herself and her sister; and she well knew that it could not be made to cover the cost of feeding and clothing another.

"Well," said Mary, laughing softly, "we've talked and talked, and suggested and suggested, and we're not a bit wiser now than when we began. Don't you think it would be a good idea to lay the whole matter before One who is wiser than we, and leave the result to him?"

Why, dear, it's just the thing we ought to do," replied her sister. "What short-sighted people we are, to be sure! We sit, and worry, and fret, and plan, all to no purpose; entirely forgetful of him who 'speaks, and none can hinder.' Yes, we *will* leave it to him, Mary."

And so, from two devout hearts went up, that night, two earnest petitions in behalf of the poor little waif who was even then unconsciously learning to cast her cares upon One who was able to help her bear them.

Clarence went to see his sister once more before he left N———, but only saw her long enough to say "Good-bye," and whisper a word or two of assurance that it would not be very many years before they would meet again, to spend the rest of their lives together. "Of course, I shall try and come to see you when I can; but I don't want to lose any time. I shall be sure to write, though; and if you can't manage to make out my writing, Miss Helen will read it for you, I know. Good-bye, Corrie."

"Good-bye, Clarence."

With this he was gone. It was really a good thing for the child that Miss Rachel kept her so busy that day that she had no time to cry until she went to bed; and then she was so tired that she fell asleep before she had cried half as much as she had intended to.

The next day it was the same, and the next, and the

next; until at last she gave up trying to find time to cry over her brother's departure. And so the tedious days dragged wearily along.

Miss Rachel's conscience was not so callous but that the sight of the child's patient, uncomplaining ways made a little impression upon it; and so, a month after Clarence had gone, one Sunday afternoon, when the house had been put in order after the dinner, Miss Rachel surprised Corinne by telling her that she might "go up to that Miss Gray's awhile before tea," bidding her be sure and "be back in time to get it ready."

Corinne was surprised, because Miss Rachel had steadily refused before to allow her to go.

The little girl walked through the streets to her friend's house in a way quite different from that in which she had fancied she would go, and from the way in which she would have gone before Clarence went away. She felt so sad and lonely, that even the prospect of an afternoon with her beloved Miss Gray failed to cheer her.

She found the sisters sitting in their pleasant little sitting room. There was a small fire crackling in the open grate; for the autumn was advancing, and the invalid found the afternoons chilly.

Helen had been reading aloud, but had paused to make some comment on what she had just read, when the click of the gate latch caused her to look up inquiringly.

"Why, it's Corinne," she cried, as she opened the door in answer to the timid knock.

"Come right in, my dear. I'm glad to see you. I was thinking about you this very day."

"And so was I," chimed in Mary, holding out her wasted hand to Corinne.

"Helen," added she, mysteriously, "maybe it's coming."

"Maybe what is coming, dear?"

"Why, what we were talking about that Sunday night."

Helen laughed, a little amused laugh; but more was coming than she had any idea of.

They made Corinne feel at home, and seated her in a low chair, to rest herself, for she seemed tired.

Helen was more shocked than ever, to see how thin and weak the child looked. She could scarcely restrain her tears at sight of the pitiful, pinched features, and large, sunken eyes.

Seeing that Corinne was rather shy of her sister, whom she had not seen before, Helen put on her hat, and saying that she was going out for a walk, while Mary had Corinne to keep her company, left the two together to get acquainted. This they were not long in doing, for Mary knew just how to put the timid little creature at ease; and in a wonderfully short time they were chatting away about Clarence and his hopes and prospects, as freely as if they had known each other all their lives. Presently Mary asked Corinne if she would not like to have her read some in the Bible.

" Oh, yes, indeed," said the child, eagerly. " I should like it so much." And then she told the story of the Bible she had found on the shelf in the old closet, on that memorable Sunday afternoon.

She told her about the verse she had first noticed, and how she had, ever since, tried to get up a little earlier than usual, in order to read some in the precious book. She had found out what the words meant now; for she had read the story again and again, and already loved the dear Saviour who had died for her, and really cared for her. And once, when she took the big Bible that was down stairs to read the usual Sunday afternoon chapter, she had asked Miss Rachel if she might read one of her favorite chapters instead. But that good woman had told her to read what she was told to read, and she would be doing what she ought to do. So she had plodded on, comforting herself with the thought that she could read her "own dear Bible," as she styled it, "in the morning."

It was a great relief to tell this to the gentle Mary, who listened sympathizingly, and who read again to her some comforting words from the good book. And then she talked to her so sweetly, and explained everything so clearly.

"Do you love the dear Lord about whom we have been reading, Corinne?" she asked, softly, closing the Bible.

"Yes, I do, Miss Mary," answered the child, reverently. "I loved him as soon as I read about him in the good book. And ever since I read that beautiful verse about casting all our cares on him, I've tried to cast mine on him. For sometimes I feel so weak and sick that I think I will just fall down; and I ask him to take some of my cares, and help me to bear them."

"Repeat that verse, Corinne," said Mary. "I love it too."

"'Casting all your care upon him; for he careth for you,'" repeated the child.

Helen had entered the room while she was doing so, but Corinne did not notice her. She just kept on repeat-

ing the verse over and over again, as if she did not know
what she was doing.    The last time the words were only
whispered ; and, to Mary's alarm, the little girl's head
dropped on her bosom, and she would have fallen to the
floor, had not Helen caught her.

"Oh, Helen, what is the matter with her?"

"She has fainted.    I guess she will be all right by-and-
by.    The poor little thing is overworked and underfed.
I declare it's a shame."

They applied such remedies as suggested themselves,
and at length Corinne regained consciousness; but she was
so weak, and looked so ill, that Helen said she should not
leave them that night.    She quickly undressed the little
girl, and made her comfortable in bed, telling her that
she meant her to stay there until she was better, and that
she was going to tell Miss Rachel why she did not come
home.

Corinne soon dropped off into a heavy sleep; and Helen,
promising to "be back in next to no time," hurried out
on her errand.    "Of course," she thought, "the child is
only tired out.    She will be better in the morning."

She found Miss Penrose in a very unpleasant mood,
because of Corinne's long absence; but the woman was

quite " taken aback," to use her own expression, when she heard how matters stood, especially since her conscience told her that Corinne's illness could be traced to her door. She made no objection, when Helen Gray told her that the child should stay with her until she was quite well. Indeed, she seemed really pleased at the arrangement, as it would relieve her.

# CHAPTER VIII.

### CORINNE'S ILLNESS.

WHEN morning came it found our little friend in a high fever, and moaning and groaning as if in great pain.

Helen, now thoroughly alarmed, hastened to call in Dr. Barrett. When he saw the child he shook his head gravely.

"She is in for a long and severe spell, my dear. Who is she?"

"Why, she's Clarence Burton's little sister."

"Well, she had better be sent to the hospital," said the doctor, looking up from the prescription he was writing.

"No, indeed; we wouldn't think of such a thing," cried Helen, indignantly.

"Well, well; it's all right—just as you like; and anyway, I hardly think it would be safe to move her now. I'll be in to see her again this afternoon." And the good old doctor hurried away.

Instead of growing better, Corinne grew worse, and

when the doctor came in the afternoon he said that her illness would go hard with her, for she was so very weak.

"You don't think she will die; do you, doctor?" inquired Helen; and Mary listened anxiously for his reply. This little patient, motherless creature had, all unwittingly, appealed strongly to their sympathies.

"I can't say whether she will die or not; that is with one wiser than I. I do know that she is very ill; but young people can stand a good deal of sickness and come out all right in the end. We'll do all we can for her, and hope for the best."

Having given directions as to what was to be done, Dr. Barrett turned to go. Pausing with his hand on the door knob, he said:

"You needn't bother about the bill, girls. I shall come as often as I think best and do as I please about the pay, you know. If you can take the responsibility of nursing this child, I guess I can afford to do the prescribing. Oh, you needn't thank me," he added, as the sisters looked at him in grateful astonishment; "I only mean that you two sha'n't have all the credit of being good." And away went the kind-hearted old gentleman, before they had time to say a word.

When Clarence left N——— he was quite sanguine as to his prospects of getting a situation.  He carried in his pocket a precious bit of paper, given him by his late employer, Dr. Barrett, which read as follows:

"The bearer of this is an honest, industrious boy, and deserving of any kindness that may be shown him.
"H. M. BARRETT, M. D."

That he, Clarence Burton, should ever possess such a document had been far from his thoughts at one time. And it was partly this that made him feel, as the train sped along, that no place on earth had any difficulties that he could not surmount.

Another thing that gave him confidence was the fact that he was going to a new place, amid new scenes, and among new people—people who did not know him as "old Jim Burton's boy."

He felt that he had the same chance to succeed now that any other respectable, ambitious boy had, and this made him feel particularly hopeful.

But when he found himself, with his small bundle, fairly adrift in the busy streets of the city of L———, and when he had inquired at several stores for work, and had been told that "no help" was "wanted," he began to realize that it was not such an easy thing to get "a place," even where people knew nothing about him except what his recommendation told them.

For more than a week he walked about, trying place after place, but no work could he get except an occasional horse to hold or a message to carry. In this way he managed to earn enough from day to day to pay for a bed in some cheap lodging house and to buy a bit of bread and cheese.

One morning, as he was walking slowly and disconsolately along a busy thoroughfare, looking wistfully in at the doors of the stores, a gentleman in a large wholesale shoe establishment called to him:

"Here, boy, take this letter and mail it for me"; at the same time adding, "Mind, be careful and don't lose it; that's an important letter."

"I'll be careful, sir," answered the boy, promptly running off on his errand.

He was back almost in a moment, and asked the gen- if he did not "want a boy."

"Well, yes; I believe we do," he answered, giving him, at the same time, a trifle for doing the errand.

"If you want a boy, sir, I'd be very glad if you'd try me," said Clarence, eagerly.

"Have you a recommendation?"

"Yes, sir," answered the boy, proudly, pulling the oft-read bit of paper from his pocket and handing it to his questioner.

"'Honest and industrious,' eh? That's what you are?" said Mr. Emory, who was senior partner of the firm of Emory, Craig & Co.

"I try to be, sir," answered Clarence, modestly.

"Well, do you succeed pretty well?" asked Mr. Emory, looking at him with a twinkle in his eye.

"I think I do, sir," said the lad, looking rather puzzled, and wondering if this was the usual way in which boys were questioned who applied for work in stores.

"All right, then; I'll try you for a while, at any rate. Here, John," called the gentleman to a young man who was passing, "I've a new boy for you; take him and show him what he's to do." And so it was settled, to the great delight of Clarence.

And now life seemed to the boy to have commenced in real earnest.

He was fortunate enough to find a cheap but respectable boarding place, where he could have a room to himself. True, it was the back attic; but what did he care for that, so long as he could be undisturbed? He thought often about his sister and the letter he had promised to send her, but as he had had no good news to tell, he had been unwilling to write. He intended to do so, however, when he was installed in his new situation, but delayed still until he should be *well* settled; and so the days rolled by, and the letter was not written.

Then, too, he had found his way to a night school, and this, with his duties during the day, really left him but little time to be otherwise employed.

When he did write, his letter found Corinne in the worst of her illness, and the letter which had been brought by Miss Rachel was laid aside, with hardly a glance, by Helen. She was too busy and anxious to think about Clarence or any one else, just then; and as for Corinne, she was delirious the best part of her time. She called for her brother; she lived over again her life in the cottage; then she was with Miss Rachel; again she would repeat over her favorite text, "Casting all your care upon him; for he careth for you."

Clarence, of course, knew nothing of all this. He won-
F

dered because he received no answer to the letter that had cost him so much pains to write, for he was no skilled penman.

He thought, however, that Miss Rachel Penrose, whom he knew did not entertain the most friendly feelings in the world toward him, had intercepted the letter. He was sure that Corinne had not received it.

"Never mind," he would say to himself; "I'll have Corrie all to myself, some day. But," he would add, wistfully, "I'd like so much to hear from her."

He gave his employers no cause to regret having taken him into the store. Quick, obliging, and polite, he seldom received a sharp word.

He was no special favorite, though, with the boys with whom he came in contact, either about the store or at his boarding place, which was fortunate for him. They found him altogether too economical to suit their fancy, so they contented themselves with calling him names and poking fun at him, all of which Clarence endured good-naturedly. He never refused to do any of them a good turn when it was in his power to do so, but steadily refused to join them in their nightly frolics, he preferring, after his work was done, to go to his humble quarters, eat his supper, tidy up, and go to his beloved night school. where he was doing well with his studies.

And so the winter passed, and still he heard nothing from Corinne. At last he gave up looking for a letter from her, and settled down with the determination to work as hard as he could and save as much of his modest earnings as he was able after keeping himself supplied with plain, comfortable clothing, and paying his board. His wages were small, and the reader may guess that his pile of savings did not grow very fast. However, he was made out of the stuff that was bound to succeed if there was any such thing as success to be found.

Very differently was the time passing with Corinne, whom we left in the midst of the fever which came so near depriving her of life.

Never had child more faithful nurses and nursing than had this orphaned girl.

While Helen was forced to be absent during the day, attending to her school duties, Mary was at home, and, strange to say, seemed in better health than she had been for a long time.

Instead of giving way under the strain of nursing the sick child every day, she seemed to gain strength.

When Helen came home in the afternoon, she relieved her sister entirely, sitting up nearly every night while Mary took needed rest. Dr. Barrett was as attentive to the little waif as he could have been to the child of the most high-born lady in the land; and, really, it would have been very ungrateful in Corinne if she had not pulled through after all the care she had.

# CHAPTER IX.

## THE LETTER.

MISS RACHEL PENROSE had been, once or twice, to see the little girl, when the fever was at its height, and had been much dismayed at the turn things had taken. She declared that she couldn't, for the life of her, tell what made the child sick. She was "sure it wasn't the little bit of work she did"; she was equally sure that it was "not for want of proper food"; and as for religious training, she was satisfied that she had had the best.

Helen said nothing to all this, but looked indignant.

Miss Rachel kept on with a self-satisfied air: "A body never gets any thanks for raising other folks' children. What with the worry and bother of teaching *them* to work as didn't know clean from dirty; and the toil of making *them* read the Bible as was little better than heathen," she'd "had enough."

"Suppose, then, you give Corinne to me, in case she should recover," suggested Helen.

"I've a good mind to do it," replied Miss Rachel, coolly; "but there's her victuals and clothes as I've found her. I'll lose all that; not to say anything about the trouble I took a-showing her how to do things."

This was more than Helen could stand, and her eyes sparkled angrily as she said, as calmly as she could: "I should say that the child had done enough, since she came to you, to more than pay you for what you have given her, to say the least———."

What more she would have said was not said to Miss Rachel; for she hastily interrupted her with: "Well, well, we'll say no more about it. If you want the girl, you're welcome to her. I hope, though, you'll be better paid than I was." And, without giving Helen time to say anything else, Miss Rachel took her leave. This was the last time she came to see them.

At length, after weeks of suffering, Corinne was pronounced by the doctor to be out of danger; and when she awoke from the deep sleep that marked the crisis in her illness, there was quiet, but genuine rejoicing among the three faithful watchers.

At first Corinne was too weak to do anything but smile, and even the smile was a pitiful little ghost of a smile;

but gradually her strength began to return. but so slowly that it was very plain to see that it would be long before she would regain even so much as she had when she was first taken ill.

One afternoon, as Helen sat beside her, she heard her name spoken softly; and, looking up from the book she was reading, she saw the dark eyes of the sick child fixed upon her, with a troubled expression in them.

"What is it, Corinne?" she asked, smiling.

"Have I been sick ever since that Sunday?"

"Yes, dear; you have been ill ever since then. But why do you ask?"

"I'm afraid I've been a great deal of trouble," said the child.

"It doesn't matter what you've been, except you've been very sick. We kept you our own selves. You had nothing to do with it at all. So don't go and fret, and make yourself worse; there's a good girl. Just drink this beef tea, and go to sleep again. The doctor says you must try and get strong."

The last was said because Corinne had shaken her head at the beef tea. However, she took it; and then, after a minute's silence, said: "But Miss Rachel———."

"Oh, she's all right," interrupted Helen. "You're not to go back to live with her any more."

"I'm so glad," said the child. And she drew a long breath of relief. Then, with a happy smile on her face, she soon fell fast asleep.

After this she regained strength more rapidly, but *still* not so fast as Dr. Barrett could wish, as he told her when he came to pay his last professional visit. But, he said, he supposed he must have patience. So, promising to look after her once in a while in a friendly way, the good doctor climbed into his buggy and drove off.

He had another boy to look after Ned, who was not quite so troublesome as formerly. The boy was Clarence's old acquaintance, Tom Greene, who, Dr. Barrett declared, was off at marbles, or something else, every time his back was turned. But it was the best that could be done. A boy he was obliged to have; "and," as he remarked to Corinne one day, "all boys are not like your brother Clarence, my dear." These words made Corinne feel very proud of her brother. They also aroused anxious thoughts as to what had become of him.

These thoughts she kept to herself, however, as long as she could. But one evening, as the three were sitting together, Helen noticed that Corinne looked as if something was on her mind.

"Why do you look so sad, Corinne?" she asked.

The child looked up, hesitated for an instant, and then said: "I was thinking how strange it was that I haven't heard from Clarence."

"Oh, Corinne!" exclaimed her friend, rising hastily, and going to the place where she had put the letter which had come while the little girl was ill; and taking it from its hiding place between the leaves of a book, she handed it to Corinne, who received it with an exclamation of delight.

"Why, Helen," said Mary, in surprise, "when did that letter come?"

"I'm so sorry; it came while Corinne was so very sick. She was delirious at the time; and, of course, I didn't give the letter a thought, but laid it away, intending to give it to her when she got better."

"Poor Corrie!" said Mary, patting the thin hand that rested in the child's lap, with the precious letter held tightly between the fingers.

"Poor Corrie! It wasn't at all certain that she would get better at all, was it?"

"No, indeed," replied her sister, gravely. "It was almost a miracle that she did."

Corinne opened her letter with trembling fingers, and tried to read it; but soon gave up the attempt, and gave it to Helen, asking her to read it for her, which she did. The letter told her how Clarence had tried so long to get work without success, and how at last he succeeded. It told too about his boarding place, and the night school; how he was saving all he could; and wound up with a repetition of the plans that were to be carried out some time in the future.

"Why, Corinne," said Helen, when she had finished reading the letter, "Clarence tells you to be sure and send him a letter, and doesn't tell you where to send it. How careless of him!"

"And he wouldn't get a letter if I should send him one, would he?" asked Corinne, anxiously.

"I'm afraid not," was the answer.

"A letter might be sent to him in the care of his employer," observed Mary.

"Yes; but Clarence does not give the name of his employer," answered her sister.

"That is too bad," said Mary. Then, seeing the tears

gathering in Corinne's eyes, she hastened to say : " Don't cry, Corrie. You can send him a letter, anyway ; maybe he'll get it from the post-office. He may see it advertised, you know." And Corrie was comforted.

In due time the letter, telling Clarence of his sister's illness, was written and sent, but failed to reach him.

It was not until Corinne was beginning to seem a little more like herself that the sisters allowed the thought of what was to be done with her to intrude itself. Much as they would have liked to give the little girl a home with themselves, they knew that they could not do so. At the same time they could not bear to send her away from them unless they could find her a better home than she had had with Miss Rachel Penrose.

They did not speak of these things to Corinne. She was so sensitive—so unlike a child. They knew that it would make her unhappy if she even imagined that she was a burden to them ; and she seemed so thoroughly to enjoy the quiet, peaceful life of their home, that it was not to be wondered at that they should be reluctant to say anything that would disturb her.

" And, anyway, it would do no good to say anything to her about it, Mary," said Helen. " We wouldn't do anything but keep her until we find a good home for her. So we'll just wait."

There was one thing that worried Corinne a good deal, and that was, that Clarence knew nothing of the new hope that she possessed, and which made her feel so happy. This was especially so because, as she said to Mary one day, when they had been reading and talking about these matters, "Clarence never cared for such things. I wish he would."

"Maybe he will, some day,' was the gentle answer. "We must pray for him."

"I do," replied Corinne.

"Then you must trust. 'All things are possible with God,'" quoted her friend.

"I know that, Miss Mary; and I'm so glad they are."

"You love the dear Lord a great deal, don't you, Corrie?"

"Yes, indeed," answered the child, eagerly. "How could I help it, Miss Mary, when he has been so good to me?"

"'The Lord is my Shepherd, I shall not want," repeated her companion, in sweet, reverential tones. "'He maketh me to lie down in green pastures; he leadeth me beside the still waters. He restoreth my soul; he leadeth me in the paths of righteousness, for his name's sake. Yea, though I walk through the valley of the shadow of death, I will fear no evil; for thou art with me. Thy rod and thy staff they comfort me.'"

"That was very sweet, Mary dear," said Helen, who had entered the room unobserved. "I always did love that Psalm."

"Yes," replied her sister, dreamily. "I think it is beautiful."

## CHAPTER X.

"I WONDER why Corrie doesn't answer my letter. It has been months since I sent it; but I don't wonder much, either, for I don't believe that Miss Rachel would give it to her if it fell in her hands; she never did like me, anyway."

Clarence did not know that the reason he had received no letter was because he had failed to tell his sister where to send one. Nor could he know that Corinne had written, even though she did not know his address, and so he knew nothing of the little girl's illness.

The boy was doing well, and had grown to be quite a different-looking boy from what he was when he first came to L——.

He had given his employers perfect satisfaction, having taken pains to please them. Indeed, he was a favorite with nearly everybody about the store.

There was one boy, however, who was also employed there, whose name was Sam Baker, who entertained any

94

other than friendly feelings toward him; and it was the
very fact that Clarence was a favorite that caused Sam to
dislike him.   He called him "stuck up," and "gentleman
Clarence," and said a great many ugly things to and
about him, to all of which Clarence paid as little attention as possible.

With the exception of Sam's petty annoyances, he had
no cause to complain.   True, he was not accumulating
money as fast as he could have wished, but he had been
benefited in many other ways by his life in L——, and
the old life had become almost like a disagreeable dream,
and would have been entirely forgotten but that Corinne
was still connected with it.

One dark, rainy night in March, as he was walking
home from night school, which had kept in much later
than usual, something prompted him to go by the store
and see if all was as it should be.

At first he paid no attention to the "notion," as he
termed it; but, try as he would, he could not get rid of
the feeling that he ought to go, and at length he turned
out of his way several squares in order to reach the street
upon which the store was situated.

As he approached, he fancied that he saw lights inside.

Cautiously advancing and secreting himself in the door-way, he waited and listened.

Yes, he plainly heard voices within; and every now and then caught a glimpse of a dim light flitting here and there.

Swiftly and noiselessly, down the street, went Clarence in search of an officer, and, as it almost always seems in such a case, he thought he never would find one. But at last his search was rewarded, and he rapidly told his story.

The officer summoned help, and together the three repaired to the store. As they neared the building two men and a boy were seen to come out of the door and, without looking behind them, make off as fast as they could.

The officers and Clarence gave chase. When the culprits found that they had been discovered, they separated at the first corner they came to—one keeping straight ahead, the other two taking the cross street.

The officers, intent on catching the men, called to Clarence to "catch the boy."

After a pretty good chase he managed to do so; but what was his astonishment, when he seized the boy's arm, to find that it belonged to Sam Baker.

Indeed, he was so astonished that he forgot to hold it tightly, so that young hopeful had little difficulty in jerking it from his grasp, and, hissing through his teeth, "Tell, if you dare!" disappeared down another street.

Clarence was so dumbfounded that he could not move for a while. When he did, there was nothing to be seen of Sam.

Turning, slowly he retraced his steps. As he went, he was overtaken by another policeman, who had been sent to see what damage had been done at the store. He told Clarence as they walked along together, that the two men had been caught, and in his turn he told the whole story over—how he came to find out about the thieves and how the boy had escaped him, not mentioning, however, that he knew who he was.

It was found, on reaching the store, that the door was unlocked, and in it was a key, showing how the men had entered. Clarence was confident that Sam Baker had furnished them with the key. How it came into his possession he could not tell, and he took care to keep his suspicions to himself. That the men were thieves was apparent, for they had attempted to break open the safe. But either the task had proved too much for them or they

G

had been startled while attempting it.    **At any rate,**
they had left without accomplishing their purpose, leaving the key in the lock in their haste.

After what they considered a pretty thorough search,
the policemen and Clarence were about to leave the place,
having found no serious damage done, when the boy observed that he smelled something burning.

This entailed another search, and, sure enough, they
found that a lighted match had been thrown among a
pile of rubbish in the cellar; whether purposely or not,
they could not tell.

Fortunately, the fire had been discovered before it had
gained any headway, and was soon extinguished.

When they were sure that all was entirely safe, the two
left the building, the officer locking the door and taking
charge of the key.

Clarence, now thoroughly tired out, made his way home
as quickly as he could.  But he could not sleep after
retiring for thinking about the events of the night.  He
was sorely puzzled too as to what was the best thing to
do in the case of Sam Baker.  If he told Mr. Emory that
he **was** connected with the attempted robbery, the boy
**would** certainly be turned away, if nothing worse.  If he

Clarence and Corinne.

Page 101.

So very anxious was he to fit himself for it, that he studied and worked during dinner time, just allowing himself a few minutes to snatch a hasty lunch.

It was the noonday hour now, and no one was in the office but himself and Mr. Emory.

Presently the door opened, and a gentleman was shown in by Sam Baker, who had also a message to deliver.

Mr. Emory carelessly dropped the bills he was counting upon the desk, and went toward the gentleman with his hand extended. Having shaken hands, the two were soon earnestly engaged in conversation.

Sam had noticed the bills drop from Mr. Emory's hand, and now, while waiting that gentleman's leisure to attend to him, he slowly edged his way across the room, unnoticed, to the desk, lifted the bills from it, and slipped them into the pocket of the unsuspecting Clarence, who had been so busy with his figures as to not notice the entrance of the new comers further than to raise his eyes an instant when they first entered the room.

He thought that Sam was simply looking over his shoulder to see what he was doing; so he paid no attention to him, but kept on with his work.

Just then Mr. Emory, looking up, saw Sam, and called to him to know if he was waiting for anything.

Baker delivered his message, and left the office well pleased with his work, while Mr. Emory resumed his interrupted conversation, and Clarence steadily plodded on with his accounts, all unconscious of what was in store for him.

At length the visitor took his leave and Mr. Emory returned to his desk, for the first time since leaving it thinking of his money.

# CHAPTER XI.

THE winter had passed, and still no prospect of a new home for Corinne.

The little girl had never fully recovered from her severe illness. The fever had left her very languid. Indeed, the winter proved a trying one to the entire little household.

Mary, never strong, had in some way contracted a heavy cold, which had caused her great discomfort, and seemed to have made serious inroads upon her feeble constitution. She was, therefore, a source of loving anxiety to the sister, who dreaded the least change in the gentle girl's condition, fearful that it might be a forerunner of what Dr. Barrett had warned her would happen some day, that her beloved sister would slip away from her.

Spring had now come, and the doctor had told her that if she possibly could do so, she must take the invalid somewhere where the summer weather would be less oppressive than in N——; for, he said, he did not think Mary could survive the heated term in her feeble condition.

Helen determined, at all hazards, to do everything possible to keep her sister with her, had, with the good doctor's direction, chosen a suitable place, where they could make their home with a relative of his. He was sure too that Helen could obtain a situation as teacher there, and had written about it.

But what was to be done with Corinne? It was out of the question to take her with them, much as they would like to do so; for, aside from the fact that they really had not the means to keep the child, her health was in such a condition as to make it a matter of doubt whether she would ever be really well again; and, as Dr. Barrett said: "Helen already has one invalid to nurse. and if she were to have two, she might take it into her head to furnish a third, and then who would do the nursing?"

While this was said in joking tones, it was evident that he was really solicitous for the health of his young friend.

Corinne had endeared herself to the sisters by her

gentle, winning ways, and they were loth to part with her under any circumstances, and entirely unwilling to leave her in any but good hands.

The child knew nothing of their difficulties; she only knew that she loved her friends dearly, and endeavored to show her affection in every way in which her willing but weak little hands could. This was about how things stood, when, one Saturday morning, the postman brought Helen a letter.

"Whom is it from?" asked Mary, from her sofa where she lay nearly all the time now.

"I'm sure I don't know, dear," replied her sister, turning it about in an absent sort of way.

She had been looking at the invalid's pinched features, and thinking how much thinner she had grown. And the dread of losing her, and of being left entirely alone in the world, with no one to work for and watch over, was at her heart, and she really did not care to open the letter at all. It was, most likely, of little importance, she thought.

Mary, seeing that Helen seemed low-spirited, and guessing why, asked again where the letter was from, wishing to divert her thoughts.

"It's from Aunt Anna Stone, I think; it's post-marked 'Brierton.'" And Helen slowly opened the envelope.

Aunt Anna Stone was their dead father's half-sister, and it was at her home, "Sweetbrier Farm," that Helen and Mary had spent a part of the previous summer. After rapidly scanning the contents of the letter, Helen lifted her face, her dark eyes bright with the light of a new thought.

"Mary dear, I have it exactly! The very home for Corinne will be with Aunt Anna Stone."

"Did she say so?" asked Mary, archly, smiling at her sister's decided tone.

"Certainly not; how could she, when she doesn't even know that there is such a girl in the world as Corinne? But I mean to write and tell her all about the dear child, and I'm almost certain she'll take her. I wonder why we didn't think of it before." And Helen seated herself at her little desk and began her letter immediately.

She told in her most eloquent manner the story of the poor, homeless child, and asked if it could be so arranged that she might have a home at Sweetbrier Farm. The letter was duly sent, and brought back a speedy reply, to the effect that Corinne would be gladly received, adding, that if the little girl proved to be all she was represented to be, she should be reared by Aunt Anna as her own child. "We can well afford it, Nathan and I," the good woman went on to say; "for while we are but plain country folk, we have enough and to spare. Send the child to us."

"God's way once again!" said Helen, after reading the cordial letter aloud.

"Yes," answered Mary, with her ever ready smile; "isn't it strange how we will try to make ways for ourselves, no matter how often our ways fail; and no matter how many times his ways prove best?"

"Yes, dear, we are very frail creatures."

Corinne did not seem overjoyed at the prospect of having a new home, because she knew she would be obliged to part from the friends who had been so kind to her, and to whom she was so strongly attached. Still, as was usual with her, she said but little.

Helen talked to her a great deal about Brierton and Sweetbrier Farm, describing them and Aunt Anna Stone to the best of her ability, making them all as attractive

as possible, for she knew that the child **would feel**
**reluctant** to go again among strangers.

The days passed rapidly and busily, and at length the
time arrived when the little family was to be broken up.

Helen, in the kindness of her warm heart, had denied
herself much, in order that Corinne might make her
appearance at Brierton in a creditable manner.

The little girl was to make the journey—which was
not a long one—alone. And now all was ready. The
sisters were to leave N—— the day following her departure. Corinne strove hard to hide how much she
dreaded the separation.

The future looked very dreary to her, especially with
the memory of her last home still fresh in her mind.
But, child though she was, she was by no means unob-
servant, and could see that her presence laid an addi-
tional burden upon the shoulders of her dear friends.
She also saw how they tried to conceal this fact from
her, and she felt that, not for the world, would she have
murmured once against relieving them.

When the hour of parting came, she bravely bade
**Mary** good-bye, striving hard to keep back the tears,
that in spite of all her efforts *would* fall when the gentle

girl drew her face down and kissed it, bidding her " be a
good girl, and try hard to get well and strong, and be
happy," at the same time putting into her hands a small
Testament, saying : " Read it often, dear ; you will find
it a great comfort.  I have marked your favorite text,
and written it, too, on the fly-leaf.  See ! "

" ' Casting all your care upon him ; for he careth for
you,' " read Corinne, in a faltering voice.

" Yes, that's it.  I love that verse as much as you do.
It's so nice to know that we have some one to care for
us, and on whom we may cast our care."  Then she bade
her good-bye again, and Corinne joined Helen, who was
waiting for her outside.

She had never been on the cars but once, that was
when she first came to N—— with her father, mother,
and brother.  Often, in the old days, had she and
Clarence stood by and watched the trains rolling in and
out, and wished themselves in one of them.

And now that she had the opportunity that she had
then been so anxious for, she wished it had never come ;
and yet, at the same time, she felt a mingled feeling of
half-fearful and pleasant anticipation at the thought of
riding behind the great iron thing that was now puffing

and snorting as if impatient at being obliged to wait on the puny creatures gathered about awaiting the signal for starting.

Helen led Corinne to a seat, made her comfortable, kissed her good-bye, slipped into her hand a little purse, then hurried out of the car, none too soon. As the train moved off she waved her hand and smiled at the forlorn little face at the window.

Corinne watched the beloved figure, standing there in the sunlight, until she could no longer see it, and then she leaned back in her seat, and did her very best to keep from crying outright. Presently the pleasant sensation of riding in the car drove from her mind for a while the thought that she had just parted from her dear friends, perhaps forever.

She looked about her curiously. The passengers were all intent upon their own affairs. Then she turned her attention to the outside, and watched the trees and fields, as they flew by. At first she did not like to find herself flying through the country so fast; but gradually she became very much interested in the flying panorama, and watched with admiring eyes the woods, with their green trees; the fields, with their wild flowers and fresh grass; the brooks, flowing by over their beds of stones, and the ponds, with the great lily leaves lying upon their surface. Everything looked so beautiful, Corinne thought, that she could look, and look forever, without being weary. But, by-and-by, she did get a trifle tired. Helen had given the little girl in charge of the conductor, who was to see that she was put off, with her valise, at Brierton Station.

While it was not a long ride, it had seemed quite long enough to Corinne, who was entirely unused to traveling. Her feet would not walk straight when she first got off the cars; and when she found herself standing on the platform of the little station, and the train moving off, she felt as if *she* was moving instead of the cars.

Helen had written Mrs. Stone what time to look for Corinne, but either she had not received the letter, or had been mistaken as to the time of the train's arrival; at any rate, there was no one there to meet the child. Of course, she did not know which way to turn, and she felt very miserable.

# CHAPTER XII.

"CLARENCE," said Mr. Emory, "did you see anything of a roll of bills on my desk?"

"No, sir," answered the boy, looking up for a moment and then going on with his work.

"Why, that is strange. I had those bills when Mr. Rowell came in. I was counting them and dropped them to talk to him, and now they are gone. Clarence, you must have seen them."

"No, sir," repeated Clarence, looking up again. Then, seeing Mr. Emory look at him a little distrustfully, he exclaimed, indignantly: "You don't think I have your money, Mr. Emory, do you? Here, sir, are my pockets; you can see for yourself." And he turned his pockets inside out; but alas, poor boy! From the last pocket there dropped the missing bills.

For a minute neither spoke. Mr. Emory was silent from surprise and disappointment, Clarence from dismay and perplexity.

His employer was the first to break the silence, and then he only uttered the word "Clarence!" but there was a world of significance in that one word, and Clarence felt it keenly and it made him wince; but what could he say? There were the bills, and he felt within himself: "What will be the use of saying I didn't take them? There they are, and who'll believe me if I do say so?" Nevertheless, he did say: "I did not take the money, Mr. Emory."

It seemed as if a mountain of care had fallen upon him in those few minutes, and there he stood—for he had risen—without another word to say.

"Clarence," said Mr. Emory, in sad but firm tones that said as plainly as could words, "It's no use to deny anything"; "Clarence, I'm sorely disappointed in you. But for your past conduct and the kindly feeling I have had for you heretofore I would have you arrested. As it is, I wish you to leave me immediately; and never let me see you again. And you may be thankful you get off so easily. Go!"

Clarence started, but stopped at the door and, turning, said in a low but steady voice:

"Mr. Emory, I am going, and you shall not see me

H

again; but I want to say once more, before I go, that I did not put those bills in my pocket."

"Oh, of course not! they got in there themselves," returned the gentleman, sneeringly.

Clarence, trembling now with anger, hurried out and closed the door.

"Thief!" said a low voice, as he passed somebody at the door. "Who stole the bills?" It was Sam Baker, who chuckled with glee as his victim paused and said, in a choking voice: "Yes, you are more than a thief, and you know it!" Then, without trusting himself to say more, the unfortunate boy hastened away.

Sam did not care for what Clarence said; he was only too much pleased to think that his evil works would now be free from the possibility of discovery—at least, so far as Clarence was concerned.

From the scene of some of his happiest as well as his most unhappy moments, the unhappy boy went as fast as his feet could carry him. Straight to his boarding place he went, gathered together his clothes, made them into a bundle, carefully placed in his bosom the old handkerchief in which was tied his little hoard of savings, first taking out, however, what he owed his landlady for board. That good woman was a busy, hard-working body, with no time to waste on her lodgers further than to attend to their wants, but she was really sorry to lose her boy boarder.

"He was such a quiet lad," she observed to the girl who washed the dishes and ran on errands. "I wonder what made him leave so suddint," for Clarence had gone without saying anything further than "good-bye," and that he was "never coming back any more."

"Perhaps he stole," remarked the maid, with a sage look.

"Stole! not he," cried the good woman, indignantly. "He'd no more steal than you would—not nigh so soon," she added.

"Mis' Tabb, you wouldn't dare say as ever I stole!" retorted the girl, with a defiant toss of the head, at the same time casting a side glance at her mistress to see if she looked as if she suspected anything.

"Mis' Tabb," however, simply gave her shoulders a little shrug and went out of the room, leaving her maid in a rather uncomfortable state of mind, for "there's no tellin's what she knows or don't know, she's so queer like," she muttered to herself.

When Clarence turned from the door of the house that had been a home to him for months, he kept right on without knowing or caring where he was going; his only thought was to get as far away from the scene of his trouble as he could.

Oh, what a crowd of conflicting thoughts were whirling through his brain! His head ached with their pressure.

"Alone again! Forsaken again! Despised again! What's the good of trying to do or be anything? I was born to be downtrodden—crushed!"

These were some of the thoughts that nearly drove him wild.

At last he stopped, simply because he was too tired and weak to go farther. He sank down on a doorstep and buried his face in his hands, and burst into tears and sobbed violently. He wept until his tears were exhausted, and then he laid his poor, tired, aching head upon his arm on the sill of the door and, sitting thus, fell fast asleep.

How long he slept he did not know, but he was awakened by some one shaking him.

He opened his eyes and saw a pleasant-faced, motherly looking old woman standing near.

"What are you doing here, boy?" she asked, putting down a large, heavy basket which she was carrying.

Thinking that she lived in the house on whose doorstep he had been sleeping, he arose, and in his wretchedness, hardly knowing what he did, exclaimed in defiant tones:

"Yes; drive me away from here. I'm a poor dog, and haven't even a right to rest on a doorstep! I wonder if there's a corner in the world where I may lie down and die."

"Hush, boy!" said the old woman. "You are very wicked to talk like that." And she put her wrinkled hand on his shoulder and bade him tell her what was troubling him.

Her kind tones encouraged and comforted poor Clarence, and before he knew it he was pouring out the story of his woes into her listening and sympathizing ears.

He told her everything, and ended with: "I never could be content to be a vagabond and a good-for-nothing, but there's no chance for me, no matter how much I want to do right and be somebody; there's always something that comes and crushes me down; and now I'm entirely discouraged."

"Ah! but, my boy, that's not right," said his new friend, soothingly. "If you're down, there's one above that can lift you up."

Without heeding her, the boy continued, bitterly:

"When I lived in the old place I made up my mind to go off, and but for my sister I'd have done it; but for her sake I stayed, and then our mother must die and our father must leave us to be turned out into the street. Then I came here, and walked, and walked, until I was ready to drop before I could get a place, and just as I thought I had a good chance to come up, I must be called a thief and be driven away like a dog. No; I'll look for no more chances. I don't care what becomes of me."

"Boy," said the old woman, solemnly, "I say again that you are very wicked to talk that way. None of us can have things just as we want them in this world; and it isn't best that we should. Don't you know that our ways are in God's hands? He rules things for us as it pleases him, whether it suits us or not. Boy," she asked, gravely, "are you one of his children?"

Clarence had calmed down now, and it was in subdued tones that he answered: "I'm afraid not, ma'am."

"Well, you ought to be; and you must be. Promise me that you will."

"How can I promise you that when I'm wicked? You said yourself that I was wicked."

"Well, so you are; but you're not so wicked that he won't forgive you if you want him to, and ask him. You can do that, can't you? '

"Yes," said Clarence, slowly; "I guess I can; and I will, if you think it will do any good."

"That's right. Of course it will do good. But where are you going? You can't stay here all the time."

"I don't know where to go. I don't want to go anywhere," answered the boy, the thought of his lonely condition coming back to him with fresh force.

"Oh, now, that will never do," said his friend. "Suppose you come home with me for a while. You can carry my basket for me, can't you? I can get along faster then."

Clarence was glad enough to accept her kind offer, for he dreaded going in search of another lodging. Eagerly seizing the basket and tossing it on his arm, he signified his readiness to go, adding that he would do anything in the world for his new friend.

The street on which they had held their conversation was a lonely, deserted sort of place, and the house before which they stood, and on the steps of which Clarence had slept, was untenanted, though he did not know it.

He and his companion soon left this quiet neighborhood far behind. For some time they walked on in silence, then Clarence asked, anxiously: "You don't believe I took that money, do you?"

"That I don't, my boy, or I'd never do by you as I am doing," said the good woman, heartily.

Presently they turned into a little, narrow street, lined on either side with small dwellings. About midway, they paused before a tiny shop. Its one window was tidily arranged, and the half-glass door was neatly curtained with white muslin.

Taking a key from her pocket, "Mother Carter," as she was called in the neighborhood, opened the door and led the way into her little domain.

She lived there all alone, supporting herself with the profits of her little trade in groceries, coal and wood, thread, needles and pins, etc.

She was a good, Christian soul, with a kind word and

open hand to all who were needy, so far as her ability went.

She was respected and beloved by her neighbors. In her quiet way she ministered to those who were in want, never failing to put in a word or two of either advice, admonition, or comfort, as the case required. It is not always necessary that people should live very prominent and public lives in order to be useful. Lights are burning where the busy world sees them not; but that it does not see or know them does not alter the fact that they are performing their mission. When we are sailing far out upon the ocean, at night we cannot see the lights along the shore; but they are there, just the same, and those near them can see them. So in life, lights dim or bright do not shine without some to see them and be thankful for their shining.

One can be as grateful for a tallow candle, if it is that which gives him light, as another is for the brilliant electric lamp. Each and every one fills a niche in the world, and has usefulness and appreciation. And perhaps that which seems least may at last be found greatest. **Motives will measure, and God will judge.**

# CHAPTER XIII.

## NEW EXPERIENCES.

WE left Corinne standing on the platform of the little railway station at Brierton, with the train disappearing in the distance.

"Hello, sis, what 're you waitin' for?" called a boy who had been perched upon a fence near by. While he spoke, he climbed down and came toward the little girl.

Corinne turned and looked at her questioner, and, in spite of her low spirits, she could not help an amused smile which crept over her face, when her eyes fell upon the odd-looking lad who stood before her with his hands in his pockets, and a perfectly self-satisfied expression on his countenance.

His clothing was little other than "rags"; and there was scarcely any form or shape in it. Even his hat was little more than a brim; his head having pushed the little crown it possessed up in a slanting position, through which his thick, rough locks struggled, apparently to free themselves. His black eyes had a mischievous twinkle in

122

them; his face was thin, with high cheek bones; and his whole appearance was grotesque and comical in the extreme.

Corinne's smile did not seem to offend him in the least, but rather pleased him; for he gave an answering grin, and exclaimed, swinging his long, rag-bedecked arms back and forth enthusiastically: "That's the ticket, young 'un. You look heaps better now. What's the use o' lookin' so oncommon glum—just as if you was a goin' to a funeral. Where do you belong, anyway?"

"I'm from N——, and I am to go to Mrs. Stone's," said Corinne. "Do you know where she lives?"

"Mrs. Stone's? Know? Guess I do," jerked out the queer boy. "I can take you there, if you like. But what on earth are you goin' there for?" he added, with more curiosity than good manners.

"I'm going there to live," faltered Corinne.

"Whew!" whistled her new acquaintance. "No wonder your face was a yard and a quarter long. Don't fancy it, eh?"

"I don't know," stammered Corinne. "I never saw Mrs. Stone."

"Oh, you didn't? Why, how funny! What makes you go there, then?"

But Jack's queries were interrupted just here in rather an unceremonious manner by old Robin Joyce, the station master, who, laying a heavy hand upon his shoulder, asked him if it wasn't time he'd taken himself off about his business, if he had any.

"I'm just goin', boss.   My business just now is to 'scort this young 'un "—pointing to Corinne—" over to Mrs. Stone's."

"Well, can't you do it wi'out axin' so many questions?"

"Guess I can if I want to," was the saucy answer, given, however, after putting a little space between himself and the old man.

"Come on, young 'un," he called to Corinne, who complied quickly, for she was afraid he would go away and leave her; and she did not know how she would find her destination if he did.

"Won't you bring my valise?" she asked, timidly, putting some money in Jack's grimy hand.

Jack did as he was requested, and then Corinne followed her comical-looking escort, who asked no more questions, but kept ahead of her, walking briskly.

It was a bright, pleasant day, in the latter part of May; but the roads were rough, and Corinne's feet grew very tired, and ached a good deal before they reached the dingy old house where Jack informed her "Mis' Stone lives."

Everything about it looked barren and uninviting. Even the chickens that walked in and out of the broken palings looked dull and ill-natured. A lank, gray cat was stretched out on the front doorstep; but as the visitors approached, it slowly arose, and walked off with an unfriendly air. Jack, who considered himself quite an important personage, gave a loud knock at the door, which had no effect, however, except to awaken echoes.

Again and again he knocked, each time a little louder than before. Just as he was preparing to give another bang, the door opened so suddenly and unexpectedly as almost to disconcert the boy, who was by no means easily startled. A tall, hard-featured woman, who reminded Corinne strongly of Miss Rachel Penrose, stood before them, and demanded what was wanted.

" Mis' Stone, I've brought you some company," quoth Jack, with his ever ready and complacent smile.

"Oh, you have, have you?" returned 'Mis' Stone,'

tartly. "Well, you can just take 'em back where you got 'em from." And without more ado she slammed the door, and returned to her work.

Corinne and Jack looked at each other in dismay.

"Well, that's a nice way to treat company!" ejaculated the boy, pulling off his piece of a hat, and rubbing his bushy hair vigorously. "Was she lookin' for you?"

"Yes," said Corinne, faintly. "Miss Helen wrote and told Mr. Stone——"

"Mr. Stone!" interrupted Jack. "Why, there ain't any Mr. Stone. He's been dead for years and years."

"Dead!" repeated the sorely puzzled Corinne. "Oh, dear! what *does* it all mean?" And the tears gathered in her eyes. "They told me that Mr. Stone was nice, and Mrs. Stone was nice, and that they lived in a pretty place," said the child.

"Well, don't you call this a pretty place?" asked Jack, putting his head on one side, and looking about with a critical expression.

"As to the missus, now, I don't go to say as she's so very nice; but I say—he!" And Corinne was astonished to see her companion turn a somersault; in the accomplishment of which he still farther damaged his already very much dilapidated hat. Taking it off and carefully patting the crown down, he said: "There, I've spoiled my hat!" with such a rueful countenance that Corinne could not help laughing.

"Oh, yes, you can laugh. But see here; I've brought you to the wrong place. I always thought I had some wits; but it I had, I'm afraid I've lost em, sure's my name's Jack."

"They've gone out through the crown of your hat, maybe, Jack," said Corinne, finding the boy's good humor contagious.

"Just as like as not," said Jack, solemnly.

"But, Jack, if this isn't the place, where is it? Didn't you say this was Mrs. Stone's?"

"Yes, I did; and so it is. But there's two Mis' Stone's. T'other lives at a place called Sweetbrier Farm."

"Oh, yes," cried Corinne, "that's the place I was to go to. How stupid in me to forget! I'm so glad that this is the wrong place." And Corinne shuddered as she thought of "Mis' Stone." "Is it far to the other place?"

"Far? Guess it is for you. It's two miles."

"Oh, dear!" sighed the weary child. "I couldn't walk so far. I'm so tired."

"Well, now, I reckon that's so, 'cause you don't look strong; but I don't know what else you'll do."

Just then a wagon came jolting along the road, driven by a sleepy-looking man in a broad straw hat and a blue cotton shirt.

"Hey, Mister," called Jack, "can't you give this young 'un a lift as far as Sweetbrier Farm?"

"Reckon so," was the short answer, as the man brought his slow-moving brown mare to a standstill.

"Are you going past there?" asked Corinne, anxiously, afraid of making another mistake.

The man nodded, and motioned her to get into the wagon, which she very willingly did; for she was very much fatigued.

Jack placed her valise beside her; and then, waving his ragged hat, as the wagon moved off leisurely, called: "Good-bye, young 'un." Then away he went, whistling merrily.

Corinne felt really sorry to part with her odd acquaintance. She was so lonely, that any cheerful face was pleasant to meet.

Much as Corinne dreaded to meet strangers, she was glad when the man turned up a tree-shaded lane, and

Clarence and Corinne

stopped before the gate of a white house.  The sound of wheels brought to the door an elderly woman, in a neat print gown and a snowy cap.  Corinne knew her to be Aunt Anna Stone, from the description her friends had given of her.

It was a pleasant sight for the tired girl.  The clean, cool-looking house, with the bright green of the yard about it, and the lane, with the evening shadows beginning to play about in it now, stretching out toward the broader fields; and then, best of all, the benevolent-looking, friendly woman who stood there to welcome her—to look it as well as to speak it—all this was very delightful to our little waif.  It would seem as though a haven of refuge was opening for her at last, and that in it she would find what so much she needed—a home and love.

"Well, now, Jonathan Banks, you don't mean to tell me that that's our little girl you've got there?" the good woman cried, coming forward to meet them.

"Don't know, mum," replied the man, impatient to be off.  "It's a gel as axed me to bring her along, bein's I was a-comin' this way."

"Why, my dear," said Mrs. Stone, addressing Corinne,

I

"why didn't the girls write us when you were to come, so that we could have sent some one to meet you? It was too bad for you to have to find your way here all by yourself."

"Miss Helen did write, please, ma'am," said Corinne.

"Did she? Why, that's strange. We didn't get the letter; it must have miscarried. But, anyway, I'm real glad to see you. Come right in." And taking Corinne's hand she led her into the house, having first slipped a piece of money into the hand of Jonathan Banks, who thanked her gruffly, and drove his old mare down the lane and away.

# CHAPTER XIV.

## A HOME AT LAST.

IT was just five by the old-fashioned clock in Mrs. Stone's kitchen when she and Corinne entered.

The sun was shining in through the windows, and lighted up the floor and the table set for tea, and danced to and fro on the walls. A wood fire was crackling on the hearth, and the kettle sang merrily.

The room, from its appearance, was evidently used as dining and sitting room, as well as kitchen; and a very pleasant place it seemed to tired little Corinne, whom Mrs. Stone had placed in a low chair by the window to rest. Meanwhile, she set the tea to draw, cut the bread, brought the butter and milk, and, in short, put the finishing touches to the preparations for the evening meal.

When Mr. Stone came in to tea, our little friend was glad to find him as genial and pleasant as his wife. Of course, he too was surprised to find Corinne there. Both Mr. Stone and his wife were pleased with the child's quiet ways and demure looks.

"Come, Corinne, my dear, and get your tea. I know you must be hungry." This was true; for she had eaten nothing since early in the day. So, placing the little stranger between herself and her husband, she began pouring out the tea.

Corinne had dreaded the introduction to her new home, expecting that she would feel strange and alone; but, to her utter surprise, she felt herself as much at home amid her new surroundings as if she had lived there for years.

Tea over, Mr. Stone went out; and Mrs. Stone, with Corinne's help, cleared away the tea things.

The child felt much rested and refreshed after her tea, and quite delighted her new friend with her ready, quick movements. The pure country air was beginning already to benefit her; for, in spite of the trying experiences of the day, she felt stronger and better than she had done for a long time.

After all was done, Mrs. Stone took her work basket, and her seat near the window, and began to sew; while Corinne sat on a low stool near the open door.

For a while neither spoke; but silence for any great length of time not having a place in good Mrs. Stone's creed, she soon broke it by asking the little girl a host of questions about her friends Helen and Mary Gray, reciprocating by telling many little incidents of their visit to Sweetbrier Farm, the previous summer.

Corinne was so fatigued with the long, tiresome day, that she fell fast asleep while the good woman was talking.

As twilight was now gathering, and she could not see well to sew, Mrs. Stone began folding up her work. Noticing that the little girl was very quiet, she glanced at her to see why it was.

"Well, well," she said, softly, "if I haven't talked the child to sleep. Now that is too bad. I might have known that she is worn out with traveling, and one thing and another."

She gently waked Corinne, and led her to the little room that she told her was to be her "very own."

Corinne, who was wide awake now, looked about her in pleased surprise. "What a dear little room!" she said, in grateful tones.

"I'm glad you like it, my dear," replied Aunt Anna, as she had told Corinne to call her. She offered to help her; but the little girl thanked her, and said she could manage nicely herself. So Mrs. Stone bade her good-night, and went down stairs.

When she was left alone, Corinne sat down, and tears of gratitude sprang to her eyes, as she noted the preparations that had been made for her—for *her*, Corinne Burton—who, a short time ago, had none to even so much as speak a kind word to her. She could hardly believe that it *was* Corinne Burton who sat in the little cushioned chair, and looked about at the pretty white bed and neat furniture that were for her use.

As she sat thus and thought over the past, with its many hardships and discouragements, and on the present, with new and unlooked-for blessings that threw a bright and hopeful light upon the future, the sensitive child was entirely overcome; and, throwing herself upon her knees by her bedside, she sobbed out her gratitude to the Father above, whose guiding hand had led her through hidden paths; and she resolved that, with his aid, she would never let one act of hers bring uneasiness or care to the kind friends whom she already loved dearly.

Rising from her knees, her thoughts turned to the friends she had left; and, taking the little Testament that had been the parting gift of her beloved "Miss Mary" from her pocket, she opened it lovingly at the familiar place, which was marked by a tiny blue ribbon, and a bright smile spread over her features as she read the words she loved so much, and of which she never grew tired: "Casting all your care upon him; for he careth for you." Closing the book, she laid it on the neat bureau. Then, having prepared for rest, she again knelt and prayed that she might be kept through the night; and she prayed for a blessing upon those with whom her lot was cast. Nor did she forget Clarence—poor Clarence!—far away from her, where, she did not know; for she had heard nothing from him since his first letter. She knew nothing of the chequered scenes through which he was passing, but God knew; and none can tell how much her prayers availed for her poor, struggling brother.

Quite refreshed by a good, sound sleep, Corinne awoke bright and early next morning.

It was Sunday, and a lovely day. A holy calm rested upon everything, and the spirit of the day of rest seemed to have entered into nature. The fields, clad in their fresh, bright verdure, lay peaceful in the early morning sunlight, while the trees waved their tender green leaves gently in the soft breeze.

Corinne quickly dressed herself, and then threw open her window, that the yellow sunbeams might shine in.

Kneeling beside her bed, as she had done the night before, and as she had not failed to do since she had found
out that she had a Father in heaven, to whom she might
go at all times, and to whom she was indebted for all the
good she received, she offered her morning prayer of
thanksgiving to that Father for his protection during the
night; adding a petition for help to live aright during
the day, as her invalid friend had taught her.

Rising from her knees, she opened her little Testament
and read a chapter. This done, she went to the window,
and, leaning out, enjoyed keenly the pure air and beautiful scenery which lay before her.

How peaceful it was! What a refreshing stillness
brooded over all; and what a feeling of rest came upon
the child, as her eyes wandered dreamily from green field
to shady wood! Away in the distance, she could trace
the line of a stream of water, by the border of low trees
that grew on its banks; while the tinkle of cow bells and
the occasional crowing of cocks broke what would otherwise have seemed an oppressive quiet.

Truly, on such a morning, and amid such surroundings,
it is fitting and natural that the holiest and best thoughts
in one should be brought into play; and Corinne's heart

swelled with emotion, and her lips could do nothing but
murmur thanks to the God who had led her feet through
paths she knew not of, to such a haven of rest.   Could
she "*ever* be grateful enough"?   She felt as if she could
not.

The strongest wish she had at that moment was to stay
forever in this lovely country home.   But all dreams
must come to an end at some time.   So, rousing herself,
she went down stairs, where she found Mrs. Stone bustling
about.

"Good-morning, my dear," was her greeting.   "Isn't
this a lovely morning?"

"Indeed it is," answered Corinne, all her timidity dis-
pelled by the genial tones of her kind friend.   "Indeed
it is.   I don't think I ever saw a lovelier."

"Then you like the country?" said Aunt Anna, in
pleased tones.

"Yes, oh, yes.   It is so sweet and quiet.   I love it!"
And the sparkling eyes and long-drawn breath plainly
showed that Corinne spoke truly.

"Now I'm real glad of that."   And Mrs. Stone paused
in her preparations for breakfast, and looked out of the
open door, across the fields.   "I love the country too"—

her voice taking on a low, reverent tone as she spoke—
"it always seems to me as if God and heaven are nearer
to us in the country than anywhere else."

"Didn't you always live in the country?" asked
Corinne.

"Dear, no, child. I was born and bred in the city.
But I came here soon after I was married; and here I've
been ever since. But come, now. Wouldn't you like to
feed the chickens and ducks this morning?"

"Oh, I should, ever so much," cried Corinne.

"I thought you would," said Aunt Anna. Then, having
given her the pan of food, and instructions how to call
the fowls together, she went back to her duties; while
Corinne, happy as a queen, called about her such a crowd
of clucking, cackling, crowing, quacking creatures, as
she had never seen together at one time in all her life.

Mrs. Stone loved fowls, and was always fortunate in
raising them. She made great pets of them too. Indeed,
some were so spoiled that they would jump right up and
peck out of the dish as she held it. And such a fine lot
as they were! There were stately, handsome cocks, staid,
motherly hens, saucy little bantams, and wee balls of
baby chicks.

Corinne had never been so perfectly happy before. The healthful air had put new life into her wasted little frame ; and the knowledge that she had, at last, a home, filled her heart so full of joy, that she could have shouted right out.

When she had finished her pleasant task, she went into the house with a shy, smiling face, as if she hardly dared smile, lest it should all change—all the pleasant things that had befallen her—into something disagreeable. But no ; it was too real to change. Aunt Anna smiled too, when Corinne told her how she had enjoyed feeding the fowls ; and then they all sat down to breakfast—not, however, before Mr. Stone, or Uncle Nathan, as Corinne had been instructed to call him, had read a psalm and offered a simple, but earnest petition heavenward.

Corinne helped clear away the breakfast things when the morning repast was finished ; and then Aunt Anna said it was time to get ready for church.

It was not far away,—the church which they attended,—and they could see its white, inviting appearance as they looked across the green fields. It was most pleasantly situated, and in itself it seemed a call to prayer to all the country for miles around.

And, for the most part, the people heeded it. Their work was laid aside, and they gathered for worship. Pleasant greetings they exchanged, as they met at the church door, for the work of the week kept them from seeing much of each other at other times. And then they all passed in, and the sounds of the worship within mingled with the sounds of the worship without—the sounds of the rustling in the trees, and the singing of birds, and the humming of bees as they went from flower to flower.

It would be a pleasant scene for our little girl, and thoroughly—as we shall see by-and-by—she enjoyed it. The winter had indeed passed for her, and the time of the singing of birds had come.

# CHAPTER XV.

## "MOTHER CARTER."

"NOW, Clarence, or Clarie, or whatever you call yourself, just stir about and help me get a bit of supper ready. Light up a fire, will you, and set the kettle on, while I lay the table."

All the time she was talking, Mother Carter was busy taking off her bonnet, and putting away her purchases, which were articles for her little shop.

Clarence liked to feel that he was helpful, and soon made himself acquainted with the whereabouts of his hostess' belongings. In a short time he had the fire crackling and sputtering, and the kettle filled with water and on the stove. The frugal meal ready, the two sat down to enjoy it.

Mother Carter's apartments consisted of the little shop, her kitchen, and one bedroom. So she made a bed for the boy in the shop, on the floor, after she had closed for the night; and once more the boy laid him down to rest, with the feeling that he was not quite forsaken.

As he lay there on his humble pallet, after the lights were out and all was still, the words of his new friend came to him: "Are you one of God's children? You ought to be. You must be."

He had never before given any attention to such things; but since he had undergone so many hardships, and had been so wretched, he felt that it must be very pleasant to have something to lean upon—some one to look to who would understand all his needs and wants.

Mother Carter had told him how and where to find this One. "But," he kept saying, "I'm so wicked. I'm so wicked. I've no right to go to him for anything." And so he lay, until he dropped off to sleep.

He arose early next morning, before Mother Carter was awake, opened the shop, put things straight in it, and then made a fire in the kitchen stove. When the good woman made her appearance, the kettle was noisily singing, and the table set for breakfast.

"Well, now, Clarence, you're smart, sure enough," she said, nodding her head, approvingly. Then, as she began to prepare the breakfast, she said: "See here, now, my boy. You know I sell wood; and I'd be just as glad as anything if you'd step down cellar and bring some up,

and pile it under the counter in the shop.   Dear! dear!"
she continued, as Clarence willingly went to obey, " I
just see the lots of help you'll be to me.  Why, I've often
wished I had a lad to give me a lift once in a while; but
I didn't know where to lay my hand on the kind of a boy
I wanted—boys are such trials, as a general thing.
The thought never came into my head, when I brought
you home with me yesterday, that I'd found the very boy
I was wishing for.  'All things work together for good
to them that love God.'   You're not that kind, I'm afraid,
my boy."   And Mother Carter laid her hand on his
shoulder.

"No, but I mean to be ; that is, I would be if I wasn't
so wicked," stammered he, astonished at his own boldness.

" ' Though your sins be as scarlet, they shall be as white
as snow,' " quoted the good old woman.   " Think of that,
my boy ; think of that."

As Clarence went back and forth from the cellar to the
shop, and from shop to cellar, his thoughts were as busy
as his feet and hands.   He was contrasting *his* mode of
righting things with God's way.

In the first place came the life in the old cottage, where
ve made his acquaintance, and where he had first known

the desire to be something more than a vagrant. *His* way of bringing this about was to run away—not the bravest thing in the world to do, to be sure, and he felt it so now; and for the first time a feeling of shame stole over him as he thought of it. However, this was his idea of setting things right about that time. But the death of his mother, and the events that followed in its train, completely did away with that idea.

Then, he had soon tired of his work at the doctor's. He was ambitious, and wanted something more stirring than driving and holding "Ned," tending the office, etc. So, when he came to L——, and obtained employment in Mr. Emory's establishment, with the prospect of advancement before him, he was delighted, and *his* way was to remain there ; but circumstances proved that this was not God's way.

Now, Clarence had thought but little of God ; had never cared for Sunday-school or church, and never read the Bible ; indeed, there was none in the cottage for him to read, had he been so inclined. He had gone occasionally to Sunday-school, and had heard the story of the Redeemer, and how he came into the world and died that sinners might be saved ; but he had listened to it thoughtlessly, as so many others have done and do. It all came to him that day, while in the cellar; and he began to sorely feel the need of that Redeemer, and to repent of his past life. And he knelt right down and prayed, as he had never prayed, and as he had not imagined he could pray. He confessed his sins and asked earnestly to be forgiven, and then and there gave himself to God. Was he happy when he arose? I think—nay, I *know* he was.

Mother Carter could not tell what kept him so long down cellar, and was just about to call him to breakfast, when he made his appearance, with his face so radiant and happy, that the dear old lady felt sure that things had come about just as they really had; and she was not a bit surprised when Clarence told her all about it. But the tears came into her eyes, when he said: "Mother Carter, I'm a different boy from the miserable fellow you picked up in the street yesterday."

"I believe you, my boy," she said, wiping her eyes, "but it's all God's doing. Let us thank him."

"I do," answered the boy. "But where should I be now, if you had not come along and talked to me as you did?"

"It was all the leading of the Heavenly Father, Clar-
K

ence.   Never fail to love him with your whole heart, and
serve him with all your might."

"I mean to do my best, Mother Carter," said he, reverently; "for I feel just as grateful as I can be."

"That's right!  That's right!" she said in response.

Just then the tinkle of the shop bell notified Mother
Carter that she was wanted.   When her customers were
gone, she and Clarence sat down to breakfast, with contented spirits and happy hearts.

Day after day passed, and found him still faithful to
his resolutions, and Mother Carter the same motherly
body as ever.   A genuine attachment had sprung up between the lonely old woman and the friendless boy, that
was a comfort to her and was proving of great help to
him.   He would not allow her to do anything that he
could do himself.   He made the fire, tended shop, sawed,
split, and put away the wood, keeping the supply under
the counter constantly replenished, ran errands, and relieved his benefactress in every possible way.   She, in
her turn, attended to his boyish wants, and gave him a
home.   She could not give him money, nor did he ask it.
He was thankful to have some place he could consider
"home," and some one whom he could call "friend."

If the thought did come to him sometimes, when he was obliged to draw upon his little store of savings in order to purchase shoes, or clothes, to wish that he was away at work, where he could make more money, he put it aside, out of affection for the only person in the world, except his sister Corinne, who really cared for him.

He had cause to be very thankful that he had so faithfully followed this course; for one evening, while he was out on an errand, Mother Carter met with a serious accident. There was a trap door in the shop that led to the cellar. This door she had opened in order to go down for something she wanted. Just as she was about to do so the shop door opened, and she went behind the counter to attend to the customer, who was a little boy. As his arms were so full of packages when he turned to go that he could not open the door, Mother Carter came around to open it for him.

A neighbor was passing at the time, and stopped for a few moments to have a little chat. When the woman had passed on, Mother Carter closed the shop door, and forgetting that she had intended to go down into the cellar and had left the trap door open, turned and walked briskly across the floor toward the door leading into the next room; and in the dim light not noticing where she was walking, stepped into the opening and fell to the floor of the cellar, striking her back and head forcibly against the cellar steps.

For a moment she felt stunned, and then tried to rise; but the movement caused her so much pain, that she swooned away.

It had been cloudy all the afternoon; and now, as evening closed in, the rain began to fall.

Clarence had to go a long distance, and his errand kept him some time; so that the lights were twinkling in the houses, as he turned his steps homeward.

# CHAPTER XVI.

## SUNDAY AT BRIERTON.

THE little church was, as we have said, only a little way from Sweetbrier Farm, and what a delight it was to walk there, through shady lanes and grassy meadows, taking now and then a "short cut" through the grounds of a friendly neighbor, passing beneath the rustling boughs of the trees in the grove, then out again in the bright, beautiful sunlight. Corinne enjoyed it all keenly. She felt as if she had passed into another world.

As they neared the small but neat frame church, they met little groups of people, all wending their way in the same direction, many of them coming from long distances. Some passed them in buggies, some in wagons, some in clumsy carts, but all intent on going to church.

Our friends entered softly and seated themselves. It was quite early, and for some little time the rustle of new arrivals was heard. When the hour for service arrived, the pastor, a tall, middle-aged gentleman, with benevolence and kindly feeling beaming in his genial countenance, read the opening hymn, which was sung by the congregation, with no accompaniment save the music of the birds outside the open windows.

Charley Reade, the minister's little son, often said that the birds liked to come to church on Sundays, and sing with the people. Whether this was so or not, sing they did, with all the power in their tiny throats.

Mr. Reade took for his text that morning the words: "Humble yourselves, therefore, under the mighty hand of God, that he may exalt you in due time."

This verse was familiar to our little friend, Corinne; for it was the one just before her favorite text, and she had read it often. The sermon was simple, forcible, plain, practical, and was delivered in tones that showed that the speaker's sole aim was to reach the hearts of his hearers, and press home upon them the truths contained in his theme. The earnest attention with which his congregation listened to his words fully attested their interest and evident enjoyment.

The sermon was so simple and plain, that Corinne had no difficulty in understanding it all, and she thoroughly enjoyed it. Then the little church looked so neat and pretty, with its dove-colored walls and dark-brown pews, while through the open windows came the soft, sweet breeze, and the trees that stood around cast shadows of their dancing leaves upon the sunlit crimson carpet and against the wall. It all made a very beautiful picture, Corinne thought.

There was one little girl, about the age of our young friend, who sat near by, and who kept her eyes upon her nearly all the time during the service. It was Bebe Reade, Charley's staid little sister. She had been told by Aunt Anna Stone, with whom she was a great favorite, that Corinne was to come to live with her. "Auntie Stone," as Bebe called her, had also told her the story of Corinne's sad life, and the little maiden was full of sympathy for the child.

She was just the least bit impatient, I am afraid, for the service to be over, so that she might make the acquaintance of the new comer. She was quite attracted by Corinne's sober, sweet face and demure air, and made it up in her mind that she and "Auntie Stone's new little girl" should be fast friends. Her brother Charley had looked too, but decided right away that the "stranger girl" was altogether too quiet to suit him; so he leaned back in his seat and watched a bee which had wandered in at the window, and was hovering over the head of good Deacon Phillips, and buzzing sullenly, as if it had half a mind to sting him.

At last service was over, and Bebe had the opportunity she had wished for, and which she improved by going straight over to Corinne, and reaching out her little hand, said, in her matter-of-fact way : "I'm glad you've come, little girl."

Corinne, somewhat taken aback at such a cordial greeting from a stranger, still had sufficient self-possession to return the friendly squeeze Bebe had given her hand, and as the congregation moved slowly out of the church, Aunt Anna Stone noticed with satisfaction that the two little girls walked out with their arms about each other.

Bebe's mother was dead, and Aunt Patty, a widowed sister of Mr. Reade's, had charge of his little household. The two children, Charley and Bebe, each as different from the other as could be, were both, in their respective ways, good, tractable little people. Charley, aged eleven years, was rather inclined to be mischievous ; but, as Aunt Patty was wont to say, there wasn't "a bit of harm in the lad ; he's only a healthy, lively boy."

Bebe—Blanche Bernice was her real name, shortened

Château de Goublin

to Bebe, because of the two initial Bs—was by no means averse to a "bit of a romp" with her brother, who was her only companion, for the Reade's lived "up country," to use the expression of the Brierton folk, and had no near neighbors. This was one reason why she had been so glad to hear that Corinne was coming to live with "Auntie Stone," and she had hoped that she would make a nice friend and playmate.

And so it proved to be. Corinne and Bebe were quite confidential by the time the older folks were ready to separate.

"I'll come over to see you just as soon as I can," said Bebe, as the two girls parted, reluctantly.

"Bebe, whatever can you see about that stupid girl to like?" exclaimed Charley, as, seated behind their father and Aunt Patty, in the carryall, they rolled slowly homeward.

"She isn't stupid at all, Charley Reade; and you mustn't say such things about her, for she's my friend," said Bebe, indignantly.

"I wouldn't have her for a friend; I wouldn't speak to her; she's only a pauper; I heard Auntie Stone tell all about her to-day, and she's just nobody at all."

"Charley," said his sister, gravely, "you know very well that you are saying naughty, ugly things, and you ought to be ashamed of yourself. Can she help being what she is? I wouldn't let *that* hinder me from being a friend to any one. The Lord loves poor, friendless people, and so do I; and I love Corinne dearly, and I know Auntie Stone does too, from the way she talks to her. Besides, Charley Reade," continued the little maiden, almost out of breath with indignation and her long speech, "besides, your father has taught you better than to talk that way."

"Oh, ho! 'your father has taught you better!' Just listen to Mistress Reade!" cried Charley, mockingly.

"What's the matter, children?" asked their father, half turning around, and noticing the ruffled looks of the occupants of the back seat.

"Why, papa," began Bebe, while Charley sat up very straight, and looked away across the fields. "Charley has been saying all sorts of rude things about Auntie Stone's little adopted girl; he says she's a pauper, and a whole lot more. And, papa, she's a nice girl; I like her, and want to know her—mayn't I?"

"Certainly, dear, if you're sure she's a nice little girl;

and I'm certain she must be, or Mrs. Stone wouldn't have taken her. Charley, my boy," he said, looking reproachfully at that young gentleman, who looked very uncomfortable, "Charley, it isn't like you, to talk in that way."

"Well, but, papa," said the boy, "her father is nothing but a drunkard—I heard Auntie Stone say so—and the girl is just nobody."

"Yes, she is somebody; she is a girl with a soul just like yours, and if she is the child of a drunkard, all the more should you pity and be kind and friendly to her."

Having said this, Mr. Reade returned to his former position, and the two children were silent during the remainder of the drive.

When old Bessie, the sorrel mare, stopped of her own accord in front of the gate of their home, Charley was the first to jump out of the carriage, and without waiting for any one, away he went around the house, as fast as he could. Bebe alighted more slowly and soberly, as did also Aunt Patty, while Mr. Reade drove Bessie to her stable.

Bebe went into the house, and, taking a book, brought her little rocking chair out on the front porch and sat down to read. But she missed her brother, who was always on hand on Sundays to read with her. At last she grew tired of sitting there by herself, so she closed her book and went in search of the missing Charley. She found him sitting on the top of the wood pile. Thinking that he was sulky, she climbed up beside him, all unmindful of her Sunday dress, to talk him into a good humor. But there was no ill-temper in the bright, laughing face he turned to her.

"Bebe," he said, "I *am* just ashamed of myself for being so horrid to-day."

"I think you ought to be, you naughty boy; I'm ashamed of you." And the little girl threw her arm around her brother and gave him a loving squeeze. Then the two sat there without saying any more; but both were busy with their thoughts, and, strange to say, they were thinking about the same thing, or rather, I should say, about the same person—Corinne; thinking, however, each in a different way.

Bebe thought only of what a lovable little girl her new friend promised to be, and planned to visit her just as soon as she could. Charley was thinking of what seemed to him the very forlorn condition of Auntie

Stone's protégé—the child of poverty, and a drunken father; and his heart smote him sorely for the unkind words he had uttered that day, and he would have been very glad if he could have recalled them. He resolved that he would be very, very careful not to speak unkind words about people in the future; and, "Oh!" thought he, "what if my sister were in her place, and somebody should talk about her so!"

Just here the reveries of both, pleasant and unpleasant, were broken in upon by Aunt Patty's call to dinner, after which Bessie, driven by Bob, the boy who had charge of her, took the children back to Sunday-school, where Bebe hoped she would meet Corinne again. But she was not there.

# CHAPTER XVII.

### CHARLEY'S TRAMP.

ONE morning after breakfast, Mr. Reade remarked that he thought of going over to Sweetbrier Farm to see Mr. Stone on some business, and he told Bebe that if she wished, she might go with him.

Charley had declared his intention to go fishing, so his sister, who was generally very lonely when he was away for any length of time, was glad that she would not have to stay at home alone.

Bebe was soon ready, and so was old Bessie, It was a beautiful morning, and they had a delightful drive to Sweetbrier Farm, and a cordial welcome from " Auntie Stone,'' while Corinne smiled her pleasure.

"Nathan's in the potato patch,'' Mrs. Stone said, in answer to Mr. Reade's inquiry, as to where he should find her husband ; so leaving Bebe to have a good time with Corinne, he went in search of him. " Auntie Stone '' sent the two girls off to " have a good romp together,'' which they were not at all unwilling to do.

Although Corinne had been at the farm but a short time, she felt entirely at home and perfectly happy; and nothing could have pleased good Mrs. Stone more than the sight of the children running, hopping, skipping, and jumping over the grass and among the trees.

After running and playing until they were tired, the girls sat down under an old apple tree in the orchard, to rest and talk.

"Why haven't you been to Sunday-school?" asked Bebe, plucking a clover leaf, and sticking it between her teeth.

"I'd like to come, well enough; but I don't know anybody there."

"Oh, that's nothing; besides, I'm sure you know me," said Bebe, "and you could come into our class. We've a splendid teacher; her name is Mrs. Andrews; she makes the lessons so pleasant; explains everything so nicely, you know, and talks, and sometimes tells stories to make us understand the lesson better. Oh, you'd like her ever so much! Come next Sunday, won't you?"

"Yes," said Corinne, "I will if Aunt Anna is willing."

"Oh, she'll be willing," Bebe asserted, confidently.

" I'll ask her before I go.  She'll be glad to have you,
I'm sure."

After a little more talk about the school, Bebe asked,
softly :  " Corinne, are you a Christian ? "

" Yes," answered Corinne, with a happy light in her
eyes ;  " are you ? "

Bebe nodded her head affirmatively.    " I'm glad,
ain't you ? " she asked.

" Yes, indeed," said Corinne.   " I don't know what or
where I'd be to day, if I wasn't."

" Oh, but come  now," exclaimed Bebe, " here we are
sitting talking, and presently papa will be going home."
And the lively little girl sprang up from her seat, and,
followed by Corinne, raced away to the barn, to climb
into the loft and tumble about in the hay ; throwing aside
with the light hearted forgetfulness of childhood all sober
thoughts for the time being.  They had a gay time
together, and a nice lunch of pie and milk under the
trees, and then it was time for them to part.  Mr. Reade,
having talked farm and church business with Mr. Stone
to his heart's content, was now quite ready to go.  So with
a " tight hug and a hard kiss,"—as Bebe expressed it,—
the girls separated, and old Bessie jogged off at her own

leisurely, nòt-to-be-hurried pace ; and thus ended one of the many happy days spent by Corinne and Bebe together.

About the middle of August, Charley had returned one afternoon from another of his fishing expeditions, and came running to find Bebe, greeting her with, "Say, Bebe, what do you 'spose I brought home with me to-day?"

" Why, I guess you caught a frog, a minnow, or may-be a tadpole," answened Bebe, mischievously.

" No I didn't, Bebe Reade. I caught a fine string of fish."

" You mean a string of fine fish, don't you, Master Charles ? "

" Oh, my! you *are* smart; but if you don't want to hear what I was going to tell you, it's all right." And Charley walked off with his head up, and a " high and mighty " air, but inwardly much disappointed, because he had not told his news.

" Now, Charley, don't get stiff so quickly ; I'm sorry I teased you," called Bebe, running after and catching him by the arm. " I was only in fun. Tell me what you were going to."

"Well, if you behave yourself, I will," replied Charley, too eager to tell to even feign anger long. "Bebe, I brought home a tramp."

"Oh, Charley Reade! A tramp? A 'really and truly' tramp?" cried Bebe, coming to a halt, and looking about her distrustfully.

"Yes, a 'really and truly' tramp," repeated Charley, enjoying his sister's dismay; "only it's a boy tramp, and a jolly fellow he is too."

"Where is he?" asked Bebe.

"In the kitchen, getting something to eat. He's to stay all night, if papa's willing. I'm going now to tell him all about it." And off he ran.

Bebe went toward the house, and around to the kitchen, where she found the wonderful "tramp" sitting at the table, eating some bread and meat.

The boy was rather rough-looking, but appeared to be good-natured; and his clothing, though coarse and plain, was whole and clean. He was by no means what Bebe considered a "a really and truly tramp." Her ideal was a far more ferocious, tattered, grimy individual than the boy before her, who, having finished his meal, arose, and thanking Aunt Patty, signified his willingness to go to work. The work was to saw a pile of wood that had been brought that morning. Bebe eyed the stranger rather suspiciously, as he passed her on his way to the woodpile.

When he reached it, he pulled off his jacket and went to work with a will, that showed that, tramp though he might be, he was not averse to sawing wood. Presently Bebe cautiously approached, and sat down on a log near by, and watched him as he laid the sticks upon the wood-horse, and with a steady hand sent the bright saw through them. After a while, the little girl grew tired of sitting there in silence, so she summoned sufficient courage to ask the boy his name.

"My name is Clarence Burton," he answered, pausing a moment to wipe the perspiration from his forehead.

"Clarence," repeated Bebe slowly, as if turning over in her mind whether or not this was a suitable name for a tramp.

"Yes," said the boy, "the name is all right, if the owner isn't."

Beginning to lose some of her awe of the "tramp," Bebe ventured next to inquire if he had lost his way, and where he lived.

No, hadn't exactly lost his way, he told her ; as to where he lived, he didn't live anywhere just now.

"Haven't you any home at all?" exclaimed Bebe, pityingly.

The boy shook his head, and again answered, "No." But we need to glance back for a moment, and see how our friend Clarence came from his comfortable home with Mother Carter, to the condition in which we now find him.

When Clarence reached home that evening, after having concluded his errand, he found the little shop quite dark, which he thought strange, for Mother Carter was accustomed to light up early, especially on rainy evenings. Cautiously feeling his way, avoiding the open trap-door as he went by, he found the lamp and lighted it. He first went into the little room at the back of the shop: there was no one there. Coming back, he directed the rays of the lamp into the cellar. There he saw his old friend lying on the floor unconscious. Quickly descending the steps, he laid his hand upon her head, fearing she was dead. His touch seemed to arouse her, for she gave a faint sigh, and then a feeble groan. Finding that she had only fainted, he hastened up the cellar steps and out into the street, running in his haste against a policeman who was passing.

"What's the matter with you, boy?" growled the officer; "where are you running?"

Clarence excused himself, and explained what had happened, and the policeman returned with him to the shop.  They carried Mother Carter from her uncomfortable and painful position, and placed her upon her bed.

The boy called in a neighbor, and then hurried away in search of a doctor.  Having succeeded in finding one, he hurried back to the side of his injured friend, the doctor promising to follow in a short time.  He came, examined the sufferer, prescribed and went away, saying that he would call in the morning.

The injured woman passed a very restless night, and seemed to suffer greatly.  Clarence watched by her faithfully all night, the neighbor having returned to her home.

When the doctor came in the morning, he examined the patient again, more carefully than he had done the evening before.  He found that she was more seriously hurt than he had at first thought, having received internal injuries, besides having hurt her back and head by striking against the cellar steps. All this, added to a not over-robust frame, and her advanced age, worked against her, and the doctor told Clarence that he feared the good old woman's days were numbered.

The boy was filled with sorrow at this intelligence, and at the prospect of again losing a friend. He watched by her bedside continually, leaving her only when relieved by the kind neighbor, who came in as often as she could, or to attend to the little shop.

One morning Mother Carter called him to her, and asked him to tell her what the doctor had said about her condition, and, seeing him hesitate, she said: "Go on, my boy, I don't mind hearing; I feel that my time has come, and I'm perfectly willing to go. Don't the doctor think I'll go soon?"

Clarence could not answer in words, so he simply nodded his head, while the tears dropped from his eyes and fell on the withered hand stretched out to him.

"Don't cry, my boy," said Mother Carter again. "I'm just a bit sorry to leave you; but, lad, trust in God; he'll make a way for you, and raise up friends to take the place of the ones he calls away."

Once again did she comfort him, and then directed him

to see that she was buried decently, and to have her little
business stock and household belongings sold, and pay her
funeral expenses, together with her few debts, with the
money; if anything was left after he had done this, he
was to keep it for himself.

How glad Clarence was in the midst of his sorrow,
that he was there to perform these little acts for the
lonely old woman, who looked on him quite as a son!
He felt that he could in this way repay her for the kindness she had shown him in receiving him into her home
when the finger of suspicion was pointed at him. He
felt that he *never could* repay her for leading his wayward feet into the straight and narrow way; but it was a
comfort to feel that he could do something.

During her illness, Mother Carter received many little
attentions from the neighbors, to whom she had always
been a friend, and with whom she had never had a
difficulty.

Peacefully and quietly did the spirit of the dear old
woman pass away, and once more Clarence found himself
alone. He carried out the last wishes of his kind friend
as faithfully as he could, and when all was done, and the
little shop closed up, he went out again into the streets.

He had a little money in his pocket, part of which was the remainder of his own savings.

"What shall I do now?" he asked himself; "and where shall I go?" he wondered, as he slowly walked along the sunny thoroughfares. "I'm so tired of the city, I've a mind to go to the country somewhere, and get work there, if I can.

Pleased at the thought, he made his way to the depot, and finding that he had enough money to carry him to Brierton, he purchased a ticket to that place, being attracted by the name, and in a few minutes was leaving the city far behind.

# CHAPTER XVIII.

### THE REUNION.

"BRIERTON! Brierton!" was at length called, as the train rolled up to the little station; and Clarence was soon standing upon the very spot where, but a short time before, his sister Corinne had stood.

Unlike her, he had no home in view. He struck out for the wood which was close by, and whose cool shade offered him at least a place to think what next to do.

He really enjoyed rambling along under the trees; it had been so long since he had been in the country. Coming to a brook, he followed its course for a while, partly to see where it would lead him, and partly because it furnished him something to divert his mind from its perplexities.

Suddenly he was startled to hear a voice call "Halloo!" and, looking up, his eyes fell upon our friend, Charley Reade, who was perched upon a rock by the brook, rod in hand, waiting for the fish to bite.

"Halloo!" answered Clarence, sitting down beside him. "Having good luck?"

"Not yet," was the reply. "I haven't caught a single fish. But there! Be quiet. I believe I've got one!"

Sure enough he had. And when the line was pulled in, it brought with it a fine trout.

The day proved to be a good one for fishing. Charley was delighted; for soon there lay a goodly number of flapping, panting victims at his feet.

Having fished until he was satisfied, he turned his attention to his companion, whom he catechised pretty freely. "Well, I don't know," he said, reflectively, in answer to the query whether he knew where Clarence could find work: "My aunt might give you something to do. Anyway, we can go and see, and you can get something to eat. Hungry?"

"Guess I am," answered Clarence. "You'd be hungry too, if you hadn't had anything to eat since early this morning."

And so the two boys started off together in the direction of Charley's home

They found Aunt Patty willing to give the wanderer some food, for which he was to pay afterward by sawing wood. As to whether he might remain all night, was left for Mr. Reade to decide; and Charley, as we knew, was gone in quest of his father, in order to learn his decision.

"Clarence," said Bebe, after a short silence, "have you a father and mother?"

"My mother is dead," said he, evasively.

"Have you any sisters or brothers?" persisted Bebe.

"I've a sister," said the boy, in a tone that plainly said he wished she would not ask him any more questions. But Bebe was too intent on making herself acquainted with the past history of the "tramp" to heed his tone.

"Where is your sister?" she demanded.

"I don't know," said Clarence, sawing away desperately, hoping by this means to put an end to the dialogue. It was interrupted in another way, however; for just then Charley made his appearance upon the scene. And throwing himself down upon the ground, he began to pick up handfuls of chips and throw them vigorously, this way and that.

"What are you doing, Charley Reade?" cried Bebe, as one of the handfuls flew over her. "I think you are very rude."

"Oh, I beg your pardon, Miss Reade," exclaimed the

mischievous boy, springing to his feet and making a very low bow; "but really I couldn't help doing something to relieve my feelings."

"Well, please don't relieve your feelings on me, next time," said Bebe, severely. "But what are you so excited about?"

"Why, you see, I've got some good news for my tramp," said Charley, resuming his seat

Clarence laughed. He did not object to being called a "tramp" one bit, at least by Charley.

"I asked papa,' continued the boy, "if he wouldn't let Clarence stay here; but he said 'No, he didn't need another boy."

"Well," said Bebe, ruefully, "I don't call that good news."

"Oh, but you see you don't wait until I can finish."

"Because you are so provokingly long about telling," retorted his sister.

"And you are so provokingly impatient," returned Charley. But seeing that Bebe began to look a little ruffled, he pitched into the middle of his news, very much after the fashion in which he would have vaulted into a pile of hay.

"We're to take him to Auntie Stone's in the morning. Mr. Stone told papa that he wanted a boy to help about the place."

"But maybe he won't take Clarence; what then?" suggested Bebe. The boy, with his honest face, had thoroughly enlisted her sympathy, and she was as much interested in seeing him provided for as if he had been a relative.

"Oh, I'm pretty sure he'll take him," answered Charley, confidently. "Papa says he is too, especially as I recommend him." And Charley walked off whistling, while Bebe, in obedience to a call from Aunt Patty, went into the house.

Clarence finished the wood by nightfall, had his supper, and was given a bed in the attic. The next morning, after breakfast, Charley, Clarence, and Bebe started off together for Sweetbrier Farm.

It was a long walk. But they did not mind this, since they could take their time, and rest as often as they pleased.

When they reached the house, they saw Corinne sitting on the doorstep, paring apples. At least, this had been her occupation; but she had stopped, and was now bend-

ing over a torn newspaper. So interested was she in
what it contained, that she did not notice the young
people.

"Heigho, what's the news?" called the irrepressible
Charley. "Anything strange?" The sound of his voice
startled the little girl; but when her eyes fell upon the
three visitors she sprang up, scattering the contents of her
lap in every direction, and, rushing toward Clarence,
threw her arms about his neck, passionately exclaiming,
"Oh, Clarence!"

"If it isn't my own dear little sister!" cried he, re-
turning her embrace with a will. For a while they all
acted as though they had lost their wits. Charley hopped
about on one leg; Corinne cried, and so did Bebe, for
company; while Clarence did not know whether to laugh
or cry. He felt like doing both at once; but compro-
mised the matter by doing a little of each in turn.

In the midst of the confusion "Auntie Stone" came
upon the scene; and seeing her little adopted daughter
clinging to a strange lad, and noting the general excite-
ment, demanded, in perplexed tones, the cause of it
all. She also asked: "Who is that you have there,
Corrie?"

"Oh, Aunt Anna, it's Clarence, my brother, whom I thought I would never see again!"

"Well! well! well! Who'd have thought it? How did it all come about?" And Auntie Stone looked inquiringly at Bebe, who said: "Tell her about it, Charley."

Nothing loth, in graphic style Master Charley told the whole story, beginning from where he met his "tramp" by the brook. During his recital, one more listener was added to the group, in the person of Mr. Stone. When Charley was through, he turned to Clarence and asked him if what he had heard was true—if he really had come to Brierton to get work.

"Yes, sir, it's so," answered the boy.

"And where have you been all this time, that your sister has not heard from you?" asked Mr. Stone, looking at him a little suspiciously.

Then Clarence told the tale of his wanderings, haps and mishaps; and his hearers were both interested and moved.

Auntie Stone could say nothing but "Well! well! well!" and wipe her glasses on the corner of her apron.

"Just see how God works! His hand is in all this," said Mr. Stone, gravely.

"**Yes**, indeed," said his wife, beginning to regain her composure.

" Anna," continued the good man, " I believe that God means that we shall rear these two children; else why should they be led right here to our door so miraculously?"

" Why, indeed?" said Auntie Stone.

" Well, what do you say, Anna?"

" I say what you say, Nathan."

" Then I say they shall both stay with us, and be to us as our own flesh and blood."

" I say so too," rejoined his wife, delightedly. It was just what she wished; but not knowing how her husband would regard the idea, she had said nothing about it.

" Now, Clarence," said Mr. Stone, turning to our young friend, who was so astonished that he could scarcely speak, " now, Clarence, what have you to say to staying here with us?"

" Say!" exclaimed Clarence, his voice trembling with emotion; " I don't know how to thank you enough; but I give you my word that I will prove my gratitude to you, by faithfully serving you in every way I can."

"All right, my boy, all right; I believe you will." And Mr. Stone left the group.

Auntie Stone, too, knowing that the long separated brother and sister would like to be alone for a while, called Charley and Bebe to come with her and see old Polly, the cat, and her new family of six kittens.

When Clarence and Corinne were left to themselves, such a talk as they had!

Corinne told all about her long illness and her kind friends and their care. "And, oh, Clarence," she cried, as her eyes fell upon the old newspaper which had fallen from her hand when she saw her brother, "see!" And she pointed to a certain paragraph. This was what Clarence read:

"Yesterday, about ten o'clock, A. M., a man, while crossing K—— Street, was knocked down and run over by a runaway horse and wagon. He was fatally injured, and was carried to the hospital, where he died after suffering a great deal. Before he died, the man told a sad story of a debauched life. He stated that his name was James Burton, and that he had two children, a boy and a girl, whom he had deserted at the death of their mother, because he did not wish to be burdened with them. He

**M**

expressed sorrow for his misspent life, but laid all the blame on whisky."

The name of the paper and its date were torn off; but Clarence and Corinne had no doubt that the poor unfortunate was none other than their father.    And their hearts softened as they thought of his sad end.

But their quiet was now at an end.    For Charley and Bebe came running toward them, exclaiming : "Why, what a time you have been talking !   Here it's time for for us to go home! "

Auntie Stone insisted on giving them all a lunch before they separated ; and then the children took leave of each other, and Charley and Bebe set out for home alone.

Mr. Reade and Aunt Patty were delighted when they heard of the result of the visit to Sweetbrier Farm.

In time, Clarence and Corinne were considered a part of Brierton.   They attended the same school that Charley and Bebe attended, and were regularly at Sunday-school, the two girls being in the same class.

Charley and Clarence were inseparable companions; and the steady, manly course of the latter exerted such a good influence upon the impetuous Charley, that Mr. Reade determined that the two boys should be educated

together. So when the time came for Charley to leave
home and the Brierton school, he persuaded Mr. Stone to
let Clarence go too. The boy had endeared himself to
both Mr. Stone and his wife, and had rendered himself a
necessity to Sweetbrier Farm—so much so that they were
loth to let him leave them, even for a time. But "Uncle
Nathan " was sure that there was " something in that boy
that ought to be brought out," and so it was settled that
he should go. Corinne and Bebe too were so much attached to each other, that Auntie Stone said it would be
a pity to separate them. So they were sent away together
to boarding school.

# CHAPTER XIX.

### CONCLUSION.

YEARS have passed since the events last chronicled in my narrative. And now, we go again to the same spot which we saw at the beginning of our story.

The old cottage has disappeared; and in its place stands a tasteful house, with a pretty garden in front. Inside, sitting by a table, reading, is a tall, pleasant-faced young man. Near him is a young woman, sewing. Though they have greatly changed, we can recognize in the grave, open face of the young man our old friend Clarence, and in the gentle, refined face of the young woman our little Corinne.

Liberally educated by their beloved foster parents, Mr. and Mrs. Stone, they had returned to the old country home, where Corinne devoted herself to the dear friends, who were both in failing health, partly brought about by worry and anxiety occasioned by reverses, which left them, in a measure, dependent upon their foster children. And Corinne was glad that now she could prove her affec-

Clarence and Corinne.

tion and gratitude to " Uncle Nathan " and " Aunt Anna "
by lovingly and faithfully ministering to them.

She secured a position as teacher in the Brierton
school; while Clarence, who had shown no special taste
for being a " doctor's boy," had, contrary even to his own
expectations, developed a strong desire to be a doctor.
He had therefore studied medicine, and now proceeded
to build up a practice in the home of his early days. He
was fortunately enabled to succeed, even beyond his
fondest hopes.

One day he went to look at the old home, but found
it and an adjoining old house gone, and the pretty dwelling noticed at the commencement of this chapter built
where they stood.

The house was just finished, and was for rent. He was
seized with a desire to live in it. Accordingly, he rented
and furnished the house, letting it in turn to a family in
which he boarded. He had a good practice, and sent
home regularly to Brierton every penny he could spare.

Thus, by the exertions of their two adopted children,
the feeble couple lived in peace and comfort, enjoying the
fruits of their labors. Truly, the bread they had " cast
upon the waters " had, after many days, returned.

They dearly loved the tall, broad-shouldered young
doctor, who took advantage of every opportunity to
spend a few days with them ; but they considered Corinne
their " sunbeam." And this she really was. No trouble,
no care, was thought by the gentle girl too much to be-
stow upon those who had done so much for her and her
dear brother.

Changes, too, the years have brought to the Reade
household. Mr. Reade is still pastor of the little church
at Brierton. Aunt Patty, long since passed away ; and
Bebe, now a demure little woman, is housekeeper for her
father, who, in the fondness of his heart, thinks that never
had another man a daughter such as his. Charley is in
business in L——, the scene of the trials of his old .
friend Clarence.

Mr. Emory, long before, had found out, through the
confession of Sam Baker, that Clarence was innocent of
the deed of which he had believed him guilty ; but he
could find no trace of the boy to tell him so. He finally
had that opportunity, however, but not until his former
clerk was Dr. Burton. The good man was delighted to
know of his success, but regretted deeply the injustice he
had done him in accusing him of taking the money.

There is sorrow as well as joy in our closing chapter. The time came when Clarence and Corinne must bid a long farewell to their kind benefactors—sorrow to the brother and sister, but peace and joy to the dear old couple, who followed each other within a short space of time to the grave.

Then Clarence took his sister to the home that was waiting for her; and so the promise of his early days was fulfilled.

The brother and sister were very happy in this little home of theirs; and Corinne was quite proud of the plate upon the door, bearing the name of Dr. Clarence Burton.

They had not seen their friends, the Grays, since they left N——, but they had heard from them occasionally. Mary Gray was dead. She did not live long after their removal. Helen was married to a nephew of good Dr. Barrett.

Miss Rachel Penrose was still living, but was a confirmed invalid; and although unwilling to do so, was obliged to employ some one to take care of her.

Corinne called one day to see Miss Rachel, thinking that perhaps she regretted the many hardships and weary days she had caused her to endure; but she found her the same as ever—stingy and hard.

Questions she asked, and plenty of them; but no word of regret did she utter for past injustice, or of pleasure at the different and improved condition of her former little maid.  When Corinne asked if she should read a chapter in the Bible, she gave a cold and indifferent assent; and the only comment she made, when the reading was done, was to say it was " mighty queer how things turned out well for some folks, and ill for others "; which remark showed that she had paid but little attention to the blessed words Corinne had been reading: " Let not your heart be troubled," etc.

Sadly Corinne took her departure, giving a sigh of relief when once more out in the open air, away from the close and depressing atmosphere of the house that had once been her home.

Once or twice after this she went to see Miss Rachel, each time reading to her from the " Book of books," regardless of the many sarcastic remarks she saw fit to make, and the apparent indifference with which she listened to the reading; and never was any one more surprised than was Corinne, when, after the death of Miss

Rachel, it was found that she had remembered her generously in her will.

How much good she had done her former guardian by her visits, Corinne did not know. But she did know that she had "done what she could."

The addition to the modest possessions of the brother and sister allowed them to expand a little. Corinne insisted first on fitting up a nice office for her brother; and then she indulged in the luxury of a girl, to help with the housework. This girl was the one who had watched by the bedside of Miss Rachel Penrose during her last hours, and who loved the bright face of the only person who had cared enough about the once busy seamstress to come and see her, when she was no longer able to work.

"God's ways are not our ways," repeated Corinne, softly, as she and Clarence walked slowly home from church one bright Sunday. The words she quoted had been the substance of the sermon to which they had listened that morning.

"That they are not, Corrie," rejoined her brother, "and I'm glad of it; for I'm afraid that our ways would often lead us into doubtful places. Corrie,"—he continued

as he paused before a house on a wide, tree-shaded street,
—"Corrie, do you remember going with me, one afternoon, to gather chips for our poor mother?"

"Remember? I guess I do," was the answer; "for it
was then we met our dear Miss Helen."

"Well, this is the very house that was then being built,
and where we got those chips."

"Well?" said Corinne, inquiringly.

"Well," answered Clarence, "I've bought this house."

"Why, Clarence! It's too large for us to live in—just
us two."

"I guess not," said Clarence, with a twinkle in his eye.
"Wait and see."

Well, she did wait, and wondered very much at the
way in which Clarence went to work and furnished that
house. But she had great faith in her brother and whatever he did; so she concluded that it was all right. They
moved out of the old home into the new, and then Clarence went away; and when he returned, brought with
him Mr. Reade, Bebe, and Charley.

The sequel could be read without the book. But there
was a marriage speedily, and the bride was Bebe Reade,
while the groom was Dr. Burton. There was another,

also, soon after. This time Corinne Burton and Charley Reade took the principal parts. Then did Corinne agree that the new house was not a bit too large.

Mr. Reade took up his abode with his son and daughter; and so the old homestead at Brierton was deserted, and the good minister preached to a new people.

And so we take leave of our friends, having followed them through both good and ill. "God's ways are not our ways." Let this be remembered by all disheartened ones. Into every shadow let his presence shine, and above every storm let his voice be heard.

> " Blind unbelief is sure to err,
>     And scan his work in vain.
> God is his own interpreter,
>     And he will make it plain."

**THE END.**